COCOA & CORSETS

MICHAEL JUBB

A selection of late Victorian and Edwardian posters
and showcards from the Stationers' Company copyright
records preserved in the Public Record Office

LONDON   HER MAJESTY'S STATIONERY OFFICE

Designed by HMSO
Photographs by John D Millen

ISBN 0 11 440187 X

Printed in the UK for HMSO
Dd 737357 C 70 10/84

Contents

'The man poked at officials with his alpenstock to attract their attention, and the lady, her eye catching sight of an advertisement of somebody's cocoa, said 'Shocking!' and turned the other way.

Really, there was some excuse for her. One notices, even in England, the home of the proprieties, that the lady who drinks cocoa appears, according to the poster, to require very little else in this world; a yard or so of art muslin at the most. On the Continent she dispenses, so far as one can judge, with every other necessity of life. Not only is cocoa food and drink to her, it should be clothes also, according to the idea of the cocoa manufacturer.'

Jerome K Jerome   *Three Men on the Bummel*

Introduction

The use of posters to advertise commercial products and events can be traced back at least to Ancient Greek times: it was much increased, of course, by the development of printing in the fifteenth century. The developments towards a consumer society in England in the eighteenth century were accompanied by increasing use of advertisements of all kinds, and by increasing disparagement of the art of advertising, or 'puffing' as it was often termed. The growth of advertising during the eighteenth century and the industrial revolution has often been linked with the growth of newspapers in the period, although this may be because newspapers have survived much more readily than have posters and handbills, which were certainly used extensively. The imposition of a duty on advertisements in newspapers in 1797, and advertisers' increasing frustration at the constraints imposed by newspapers (which continued to insist that all advertisements should be confined to a single column), meant that by the early nineteenth century posters were being used more than ever before.

The growth of an urban society in the course of the nineteenth century, however, brought mass advertising on a scale hitherto unknown. Already by 1851 the census classified over half the British population of 27 million people as 'urban'. By 1911 there were over 40 million people, and four fifths of them were in urban areas, where advertisers could reach them easily with bill posters. Further, the standard of living of the bulk of the British population rose in the late nineteenth century, and families had more money to spend on a variety of goods and services.

The major priorities in family budgets were food, clothing and housing: expenditure on all three increased in the late nineteenth century and more and more people could choose precisely how they spent their money on such basics. Once they were freed from a concern with mere subsistence, people sought more and better food and clothing and a higher standard of housing and household goods. They also had a larger surplus to spend on luxuries and on leisure and entertainment. Industries such as food processing, and clothes and household goods manufacture were transformed to produce new and better products to meet those new demands. New kinds of retailing were developed, and whole industries arose to satisfy the demand for entertainment. New advertising and sales techniques were introduced to stimulate the growing demand still further. Entrepreneurs were prepared to spend vast amounts on advertising campaigns, and were aided by technological developments. Advances in printing technology, particularly the development of chromolithography in the 1870s, made it possible for the first time to produce cheaply large numbers of illustrated posters in colour.

These social, economic and technological developments brought in their train the growth of what we now term the advertising industry. By 1877 it was estimated that there were over two hundred bill posters working in London alone, and advertising contractors were established all over the country in even quite small towns. The huge numbers of posters led to sustained criticism in newspapers of 'the horrors of the walls', although Oscar Wilde felt that street advertising 'brought colour into the drab monotony of English streets'. The United Kingdom Billposters Association, founded by Edward Sheldon of Leeds in 1862, attempted to regulate the industry and initiated protected sites. The erection of signs and hoardings on particularly prominent and beautiful sites, however, aroused much hostility. The highly vocal National Society for the Checking the Abuse of Public Advertising – known as SCAPA – led a campaign which culminated in 1907 in the Advertisements Regulation Act, which empowered local authorities to make bye-laws regulating hoardings and protecting amenities. This did succeed in checking the worst abuses.

Attempts were also made to control the content and tone of posters. Following the passage of the Indecent Advertisements Act in 1889 and the prosecution of a poster depicting a female acrobat in flesh-coloured tights, the Billposters' Association established a censorship committee. As some of the posters reproduced here show, however, neither statutory nor internal self-regulating measures were entirely successful in preventing advertisers from using sexually titillating illustrations to sell their products.

In the early years many advertisers had found it difficult to use illustrations effectively in their posters. Often there was little attempt to integrate the picture and the written message or slogan. Some advertisers spent large sums in buying paintings such as Millais' *Bubbles* to which they could then attach their names, while poster artists often produced pictures to which a message or name could be added. But the later part of the period saw the growth of large advertising agencies such as Nathaniel Lloyd and Company and S H Benson in London, and Hind, Hoyle and Light Ltd. in Manchester. These agencies employed or commissioned artists to work to a specific brief, and their designs thus tended to be integrated closely with the product they were advertising. Despite the growth of advertising agencies, however, many firms both large and small continued to arrange their own advertising campaigns and even to design their own posters.

Posters and Copyright

The posters and show-cards in this book have been selected from those in which copyright was secured by registration with the Stationers' Company in London. Registration of the ownership of copyright in works of art was possible under the Fine Arts Copyright Act 1862 and in the late nineteenth century companies, advertising agents and artists increasingly made use of registration to prevent others using the artwork and slogans they used in their advertising campaigns. By no means all posters were registered, since many companies did not consider registration of copyright worth the small trouble it involved. But those which were registered give a fascinating glimpse of the developing mass market of the period and of the ways in which products and services were promoted.

Advertisers registered ownership of the copyright by completing a form giving a brief description of the work, the name and address of the owner of the copyright and the name and address of the 'author' or artist. When artists produced paintings or drawings for advertisers who paid them a fee, the copyright lay with the advertiser; but sometimes agreements were made to transfer the copyright back to the artist, and these too are recorded on the forms lodged at Stationers' Hall. Finally, there was almost invariably annexed to the form a copy of the work in question, and it is these which are reproduced here.

The Imperial Copyright Act 1911 gave copyright protection without this formality and statutory registration at Stationers' Hall therefore ceased on 1 July 1912. The register and entry forms were subsequently transferred to the Public Record Office, where they are now available to the public under the class code COPY 1. There are a number of different series of registers: books literary and commercial; paintings and drawings general, artistic and commercial; and photographs. The posters here have been selected from the paintings and drawings general and commercial.

Many of them are not readily available elsewhere and their range and the information which is attached to them makes them an important source for those interested in the history of advertising.

The posters and show-cards have been selected to illustrate the range and diversity of those in the Stationers' Hall records at the Public Record Office. They are not a strictly representative sample of the collection, which is itself by no means a complete record of the posters of the period. The posters have been arranged into six groups according to the products or services they advertise, with a final small selection of political posters. They might equally well have been arranged by type or theme. Students of the media have become increasingly interested in the stereotypes presented by advertisers, and a number of such stereotypes are evident in this selection. Women and children are portrayed much more frequently than men, and almost invariably in passive roles. Domestic servants appear in advertisements not only for cleaning materials but for confectionery, tobacco and drinks. The majority of the men illustrated are in military or naval dress, and there was clearly a conscious attempt to attach to a wide range of products from tobacco and whisky to salt and 'stomach tonic' the patriotic connotations of the armed forces, particularly during the Boer War. Queen Victoria herself is depicted in posters advertising meat extract and soap. Some posters attempted to use humour in projecting their message, and there is an interesting example of the advertising industry mocking itself in the poster advertising Cope's tobacco. But much of the humour is extremely offensive to modern sensibilities, since it is openly racist. 'Niggers', particularly children, feature frequently in posters of the period, and the attitude towards them is exemplified in the 'Chlorinol' poster with the caption 'I want to be like de white nigger'. Such offensiveness apart, the posters reproduced here show how much today's advertisers depend on techniques developed before the First World War.

Details of the plates are listed following plate 80

Further Reading

W Hamish Fraser   *The Coming of the Mass Market, 1850–1914*
(London 1981)
D and G Hindley   *Advertising in Victorian England, 1837–1901*
(London 1972)
H F Hutchinson   *The Poster, an Illustrated History from 1860* (London 1968)
T R Nevett   *Advertising in Britain: A History* (London 1982)
Cyril Sheldon   *A History of Poster Advertising* (London 1937)

Food and Drink

Food and drink were the most extensively advertised products and the most important call on family budgets. The posters reproduced here reflect a number of important developments in the late nineteenth century. Large producers were beginning to brand their output of basic foods such as salt, bacon, flour and tea and to advertise the superiority of their particular brands. New processed foods like soups, sauces and meat extract were intensively promoted, though not always with great success: tinned meat was regarded with great suspicion, despite its cheapness, before the First World War. Advertisers enjoyed greater success in promoting the sale of the materials for home baking: the rising standard of living and the wider availability of cooking stoves in working class homes probably meant that an increasing proportion of the family's flour consumption – which was rising – went in biscuits and cakes rather than bread.

Average yearly consumption of tea rose from 2lbs per person in 1851 to 6lbs by the end of the century, and after John Horniman introduced the branded tea packet there was considerable rivalry between rival suppliers such as Brooke Bond, Lipton and the Co-operative Wholesale Society. Sales of coffee remained stagnant, despite extensive advertising and the prevalence of coffee stalls in London; but consumption of cocoa more than doubled after John Cadbury introduced a new process for making it in the 1860s, based on the extraction of fats which could then be used to make chocolate slab. Advertising of both cocoa and chocolate was wildly successful, and the major firms of Cadbury, Rowntree and Fry expanded dramatically.

Alcohol and Tobacco

Alcohol and tobacco were the main working class luxuries, and there were also important middle and upper class markets for manufacturers to tap. Consumption of beer fluctuated in the late nineteenth century but the most significant development was the rapid concentration of the brewing industry. Large firms like Guinness, Ind Coope and Truman, in major brewing centres such as Dublin, Burton and London, began to exploit national rather than regional markets. Porter and strong beer, locally brewed, began to give way to paler, less alcoholic brews. Whisky was drunk little outside Scotland before the 1880s, but the problems of the French wine industry and the move away from single malts to the production of blended whisky brought a concerted effort to market whisky in England.

Tobacco consumption rose threefold between 1851 and 1914, but the major development was the introduction of the cigarette, first produced on a large scale by W.D. & H.O. Wills in the 1880s. Cigarettes became a cheap substitute for pipe tobacco for the working classes, but manufacturers also succeeded in persuading the middle classes that smoking was socially acceptable (though perhaps a touch risqué) even for women.

Clothing and Shoes

The proportion of family budgets spent on clothing and shoes probably doubled between the mid nineteenth and the early twentieth centuries. Before the 1870s few of the working classes bought new clothes, relying on second hand clothing and hand-me-downs. But the introduction of the sewing machine and the application of steam power to circular knitting frames revolutionized the clothing industries. Production of cheap ready-made clothing, particularly underclothes, developed rapidly. Underclothes and corsets were advertised extensively, much more so than outer garments, which were of course much less standardised and thus less susceptible to large scale advertising campaigns. Cloth was also extensively advertised, as the sewing machine made home clothes-making much easier.

Machine sewing and cutting also revolutionised the boot and shoe industry. But boots and shoes remained a major expense for working men, while working class women were notoriously badly shod. Patching and mending boots and shoes to make them last was essential even for the relatively prosperous. Nevertheless the general increase in real incomes and leisure is shown by the size of the market for football boots: three-quarters of a million men were playing football by 1911.

Cleaning, Blacking, Heat and Light

Cleanliness was, of course, next to godliness in the Victorian middle class view of the world, but the battle against dirt and grime in working class homes must often have been a losing one, if it was fought at all. Consumption of soap certainly increased, especially after the abolition of the excise duty in 1853. But the major revolution came with Lever's introduction of branded soap and national advertising in the 1880s. Until then, soap had been manufactured and marketed locally, and often simply cut from a huge slab by the shopkeeper. But from the 1880s massive sums were spent in advertising the superior qualities of products like Hudson's Extract of Soap and Watson's Matchless Cleaner. Lever set out particularly to persuade the working classes to use more soap, but the posters reproduced here concentrate on the middle class market, with servants predominating in the illustrations.

Other cleaning agents – bleaches, grate blacking, furniture polishes and so on – became increasingly important items of family expenditure as more families had more things to clean. Advertisers showed a good deal of ingenuity in proclaiming the virtues of their particular products, although the links between dirt and blackness, cleanliness and whiteness brought some particularly offensive illustrations using 'niggers'. By the end of the period, with the development of gas, electricity and enclosed stoves, the battle against dirt was somewhat easier than it had been earlier.

Pills and Potions

Patent medicines had been advertised extensively since the eighteenth century, and their manufacturers probably spent more than any others on advertising in this period. Thomas Holloway was spending £50,000 a year on advertising his pills and ointments by 1883, and Thomas Beecham £120,000 a year by 1891. They captured a vast market, and sales of medicines grew fivefold between 1850 and 1914. Giants such as Beecham did not have the market entirely to themselves of course, and there was still room for the local manufacturer such as the Kuro Company of Leeds. Many of the potions were probably harmless, and were often useful for treating minor complaints, even if only as placebos. But the extravagant claims made by many advertisers, with pills alleged to cure everything from cholera to melancholia, aroused increasing disquiet; legal controls on such advertisements were frequently recommended although none were introduced until 1936.

More helpful than the pills and potions was the promotion of personal hygiene; though one wonders at the effects of carbolic toothpaste and of starch used as a baby powder.

Leisure and Entertainment

A new leisure industry was created in the late nineteenth century as more and more people found that they had time and money to spend on simply enjoying themselves. Public houses were transformed into musical halls, and such was their success that large conglomerates such as Moss Empires soon ran purpose-built music halls right across the country. Proprietors and agents spent a good deal in promoting appearances by stars such as Dan Leno and Marie Lloyd – the first stars of mass entertainment – and the daredevil circus acts pioneered by Barnum in America. But by the early years of this century music halls were already showing films, and purpose-built cinemas with regular shows soon followed.

With more people able to make choices about how they spent their money, the scope for choice expanded hugely. In the home, there were more pets, more books, more games. Outside the home there were more museums and art galleries, football and cricket matches, and restaurants. Public transport, the bicycle and the car made the world outside the home and its immediate vicinity more available to a wide range of people.

Politics

The late nineteenth century saw an increasing popular involvement in party politics. The Second Reform Act in 1867 gave the vote to the bulk of the working class in borough constituencies and in 1885 the franchise in county constituencies was opened up to working men. Sections of both the Conservative and the Liberal parties tried to organise and represent the new electorate, but in both the power of the old aristocracy remained strong and entrenched. It was still difficult for working men to be elected to Parliament, and the Labour Representation Committee was formed as a result of a Trades Union Congress initiative in 1899. In 1906 it became the Labour Party.

In the 1880s the dominant issue in British national politics was the union of Great Britain and Ireland. Gladstone's Irish Home Rule Bill split the Liberal party in 1886, and thus led to its defeat in the election of that year. Ireland was a major issue again in the election of 1892, which the Liberals won, but the defeat of a new Home Rule Bill and Gladstone's resignation in 1894 left the Liberals disunited again. This and a rising tide of imperialism, expressed in the 'scramble for Africa', brought a Conservative victory in the election in 1895, and a Unionist government led by Lord Salisbury, with his nephew Arthur Balfour as leader in the Commons. Joseph Chamberlain, who had defected with other 'Liberal Unionists' from the Liberal party in 1886, was Colonial Secretary. Chamberlain was keen to introduce some measures of social reform, but imperial commitments prevented his achieving very much: the expense of the South African War meant that a scheme for old age pensions had to be put aside.

The outbreak of the Boer War in 1899 was followed by a series of military disasters for the British forces, due largely to inept leadership by General Buller. The dispatch in early 1900 of Lord Roberts as Commander-in-Chief and Kitchener as Chief of Staff, however, brought a rapid improvement. Bloemfontein was occupied in March, Mafeking was relieved in May and Pretoria, capital of the Transvaal, was captured on 5 June. Lord Roberts became a national hero. Salisbury seized the opportunity to call an election in October 1900 and it is from that election campaign that the first three posters emanate. The election caught the Liberals once more divided and ill-prepared; many had embraced imperialism, and these Liberal Imperialists did their best to thwart the

Gladstonian 'Little Englanders' or 'pro-Boers'. Henry Campbell-Bannerman, the party leader who sat uneasily between the two wings of the party, held it together only with great difficulty. The 1900 election has often been dubbed the 'Khaki Election': Chamberlain especially tried to exploit wartime patriotic fervour. The main emphasis of the Unionist campaign, however, was on Liberal disunity and it was no surprise that the election brought a Conservative majority of 134. Only two of the fifteen candidates of the Labour Representation Committee were elected.

At a local level, national politics often intermeshed with more immediate municipal concerns. The London County Council, like other county councils, was established in 1888, and its triennial elections were keenly contested. Water and sanitation were major municipal issues, and the London County Council tried four times in the late 1890s to obtain powers to purchase the undertakings of the eight companies which supplied water to London. A Royal Commission was established in 1897 under Lord Llandaff, which recommended that all London water undertakings be concentrated in one authority. This recommendation led to the establishment of the Metropolitan Water Board in 1903. The last poster in this section illustrates the campaign against the London water companies in the late 1890s.

The Plates

1 Edwards' Desiccated Soup
Date registered: 19 September 1900
Size: 26cm x 33cm

2 Holbrook's Sauce
Date registered: 4 November 1898
Size: 20cm x 29cm

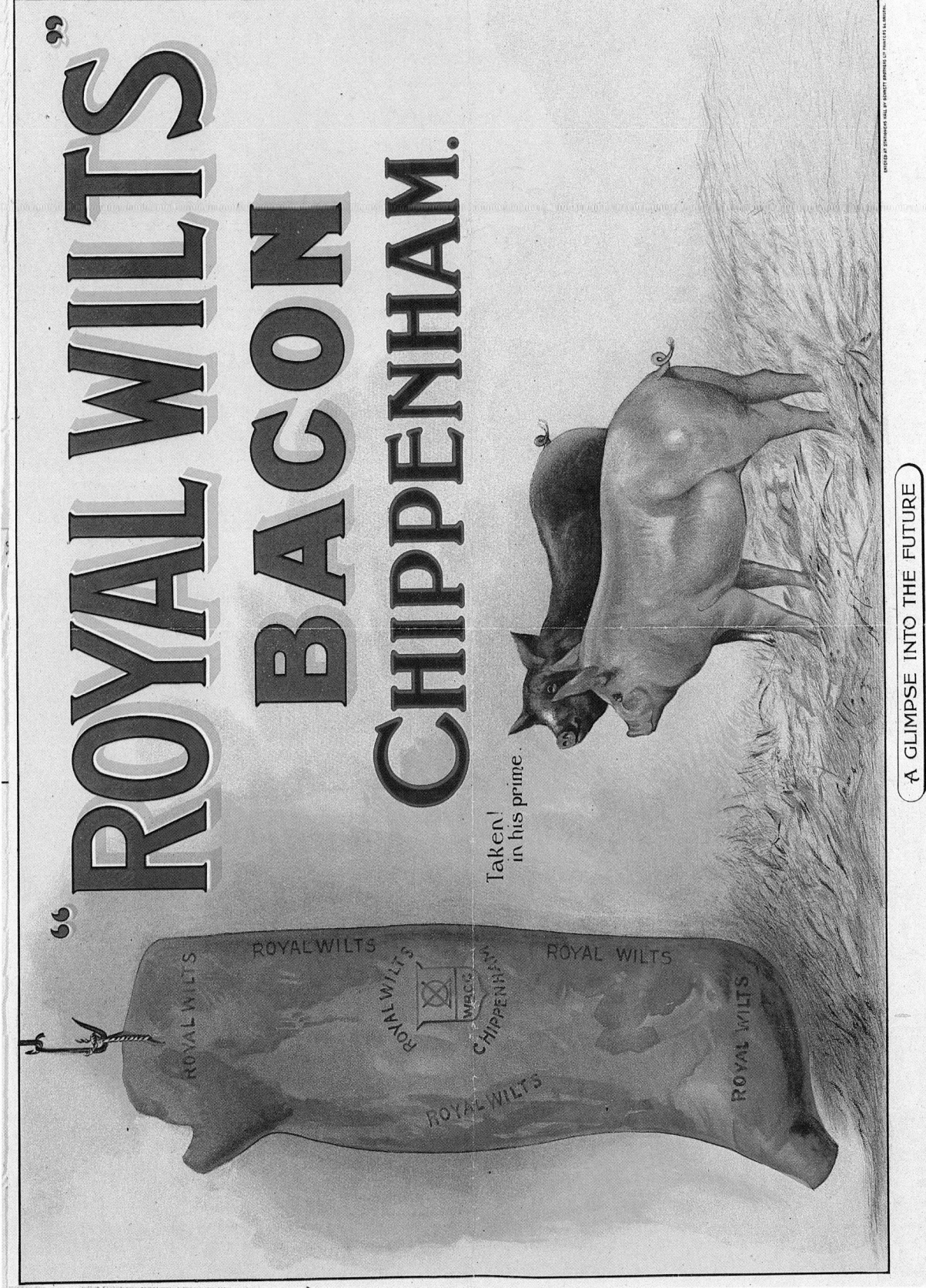

3 Royal Wilts Bacon
Date registered: 8 January 1908
Size: 53cm x 38cm

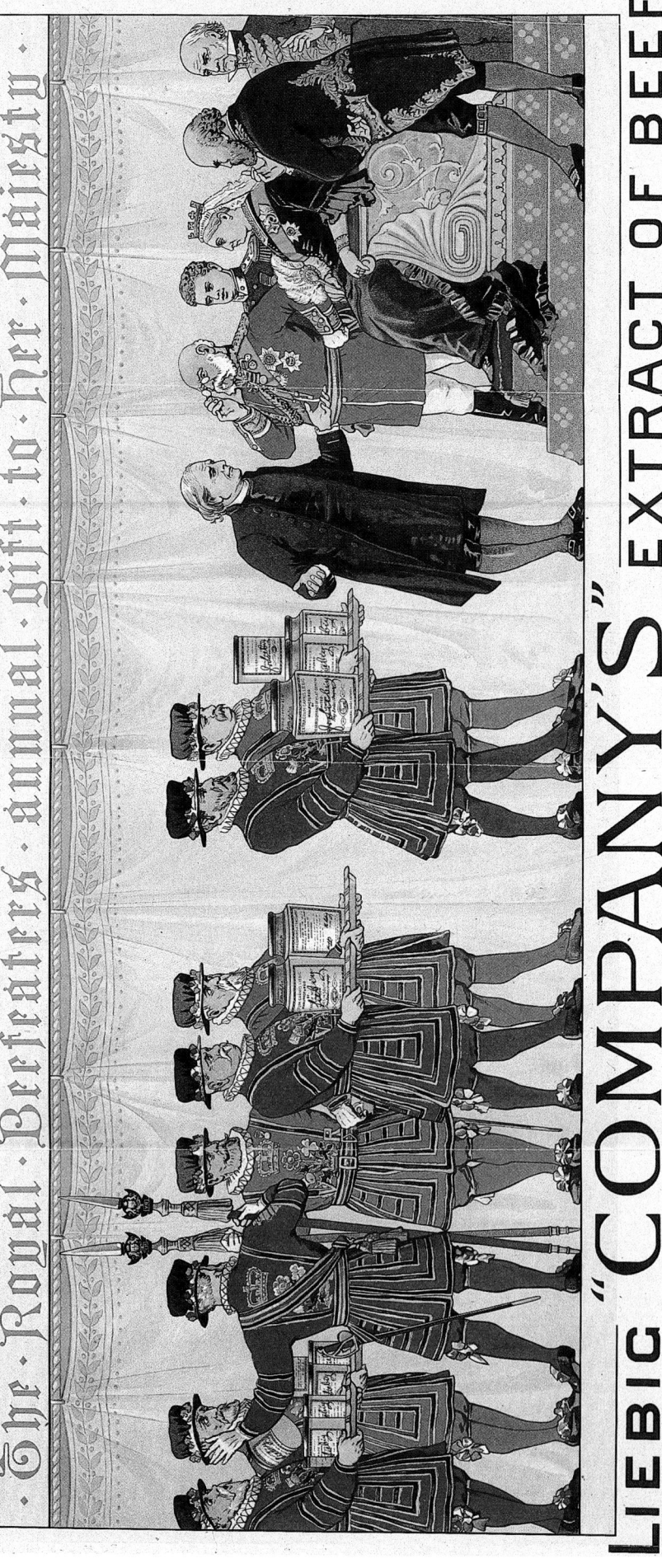

SEE THAT THE SIGNATURE *Liebig* IN BLUE IS ON EACH JAR

The · Royal · Beefeaters · annual · gift · to · Her · Majesty ·

LIEBIG "COMPANY'S" EXTRACT OF BEEF

4 Liebig's Extract of Meat
Date registered: 30 August 1888
Size: 58 x 30cm

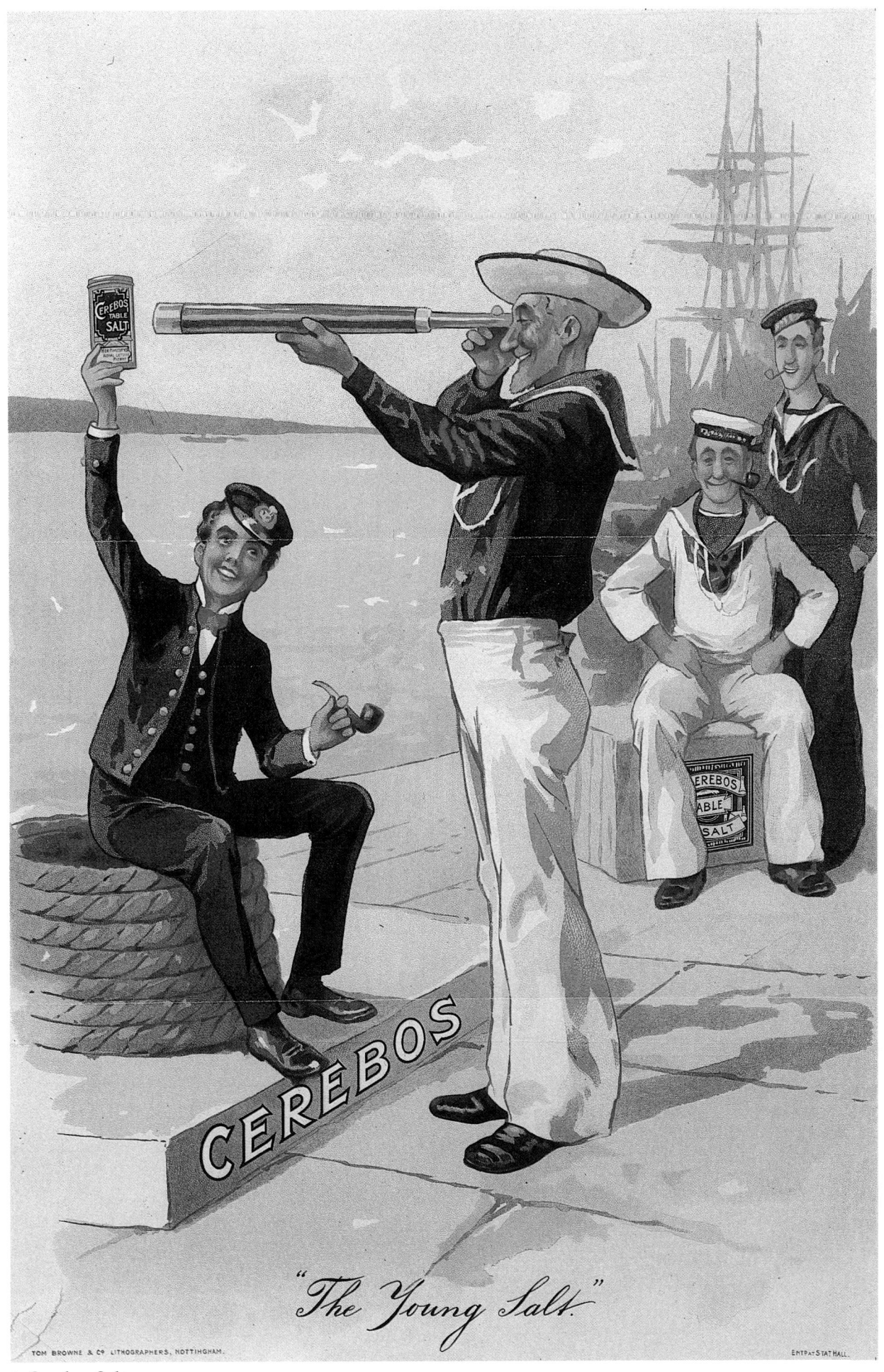

"The Young Salt."

TOM BROWNE & Cº LITHOGRAPHERS, NOTTINGHAM.

EHTPAT STAT HALL.

5 Cerebos Salt
Date registered: 19 December 1898
Size: 26cm x 39xm

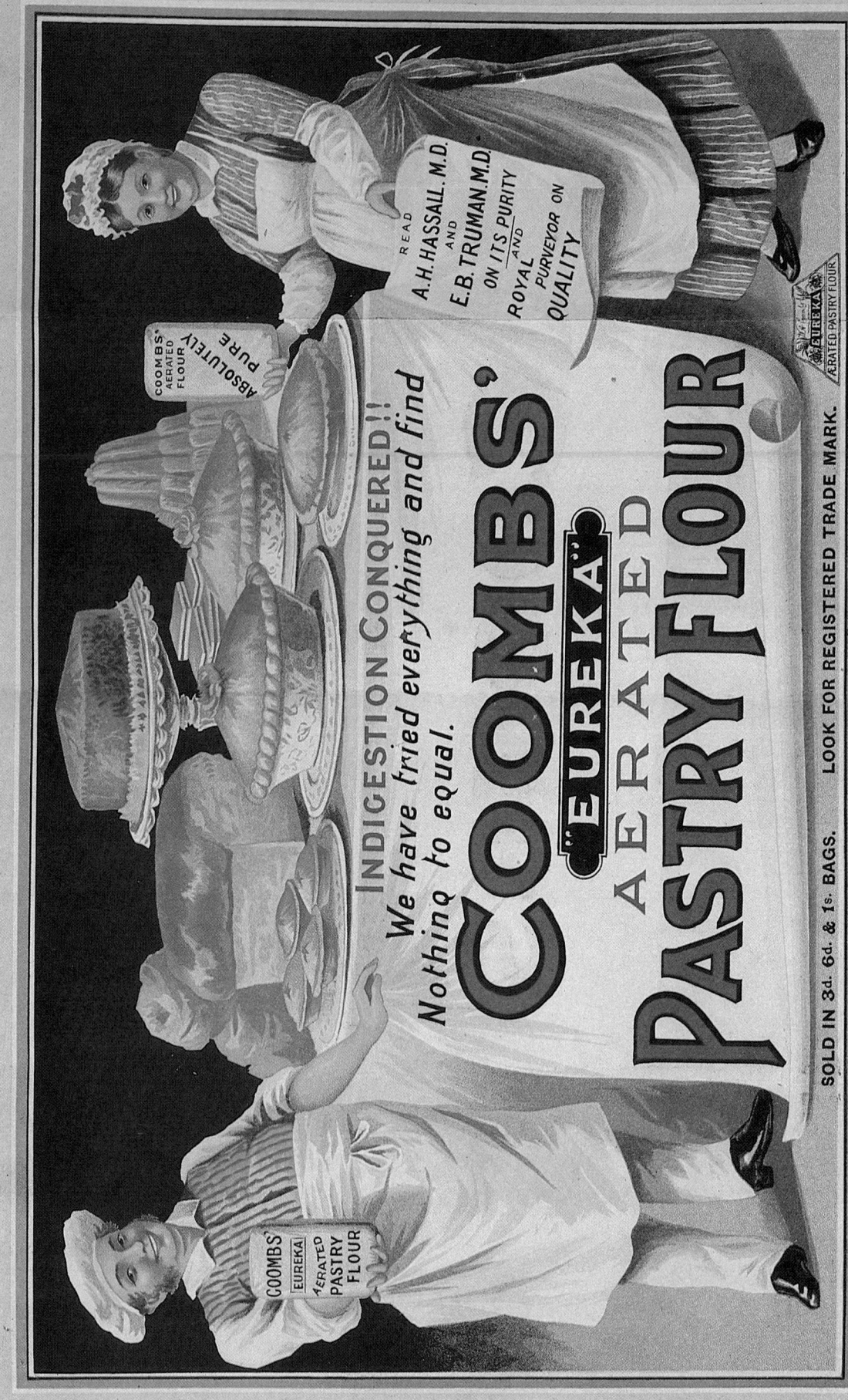

6 Coomb's Eureka Aerated Pastry Flour
Date registered: 11 May 1888
Size: 37cm x 24cm

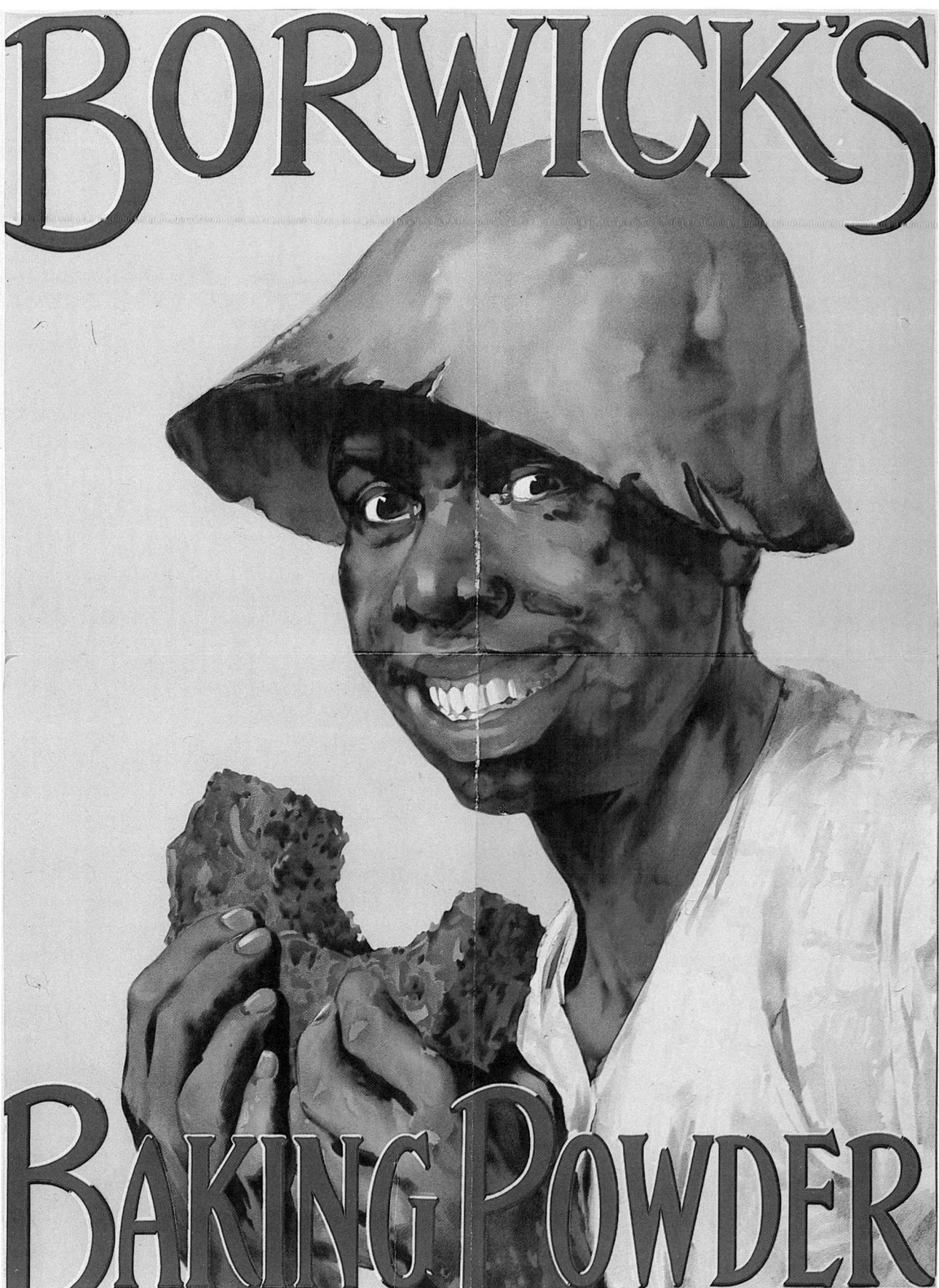

7 Borwick's Baking Powder
Date registered: 25 July 1898
Size: 39cm x 52cm

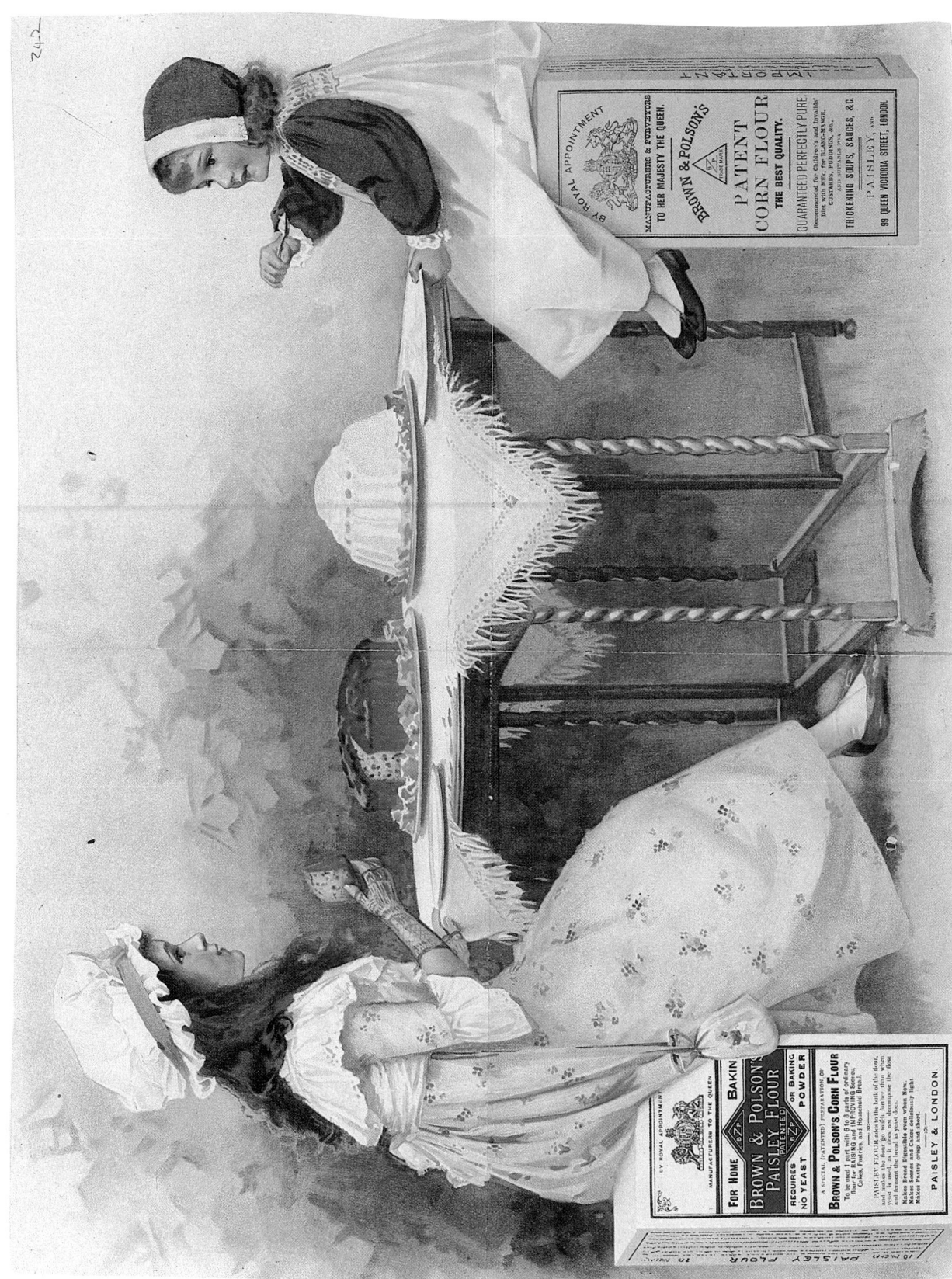

8 Brown and Polson's Corn Flour
Date registered: 9 August 1900
Size: 51 cm x 39 cm

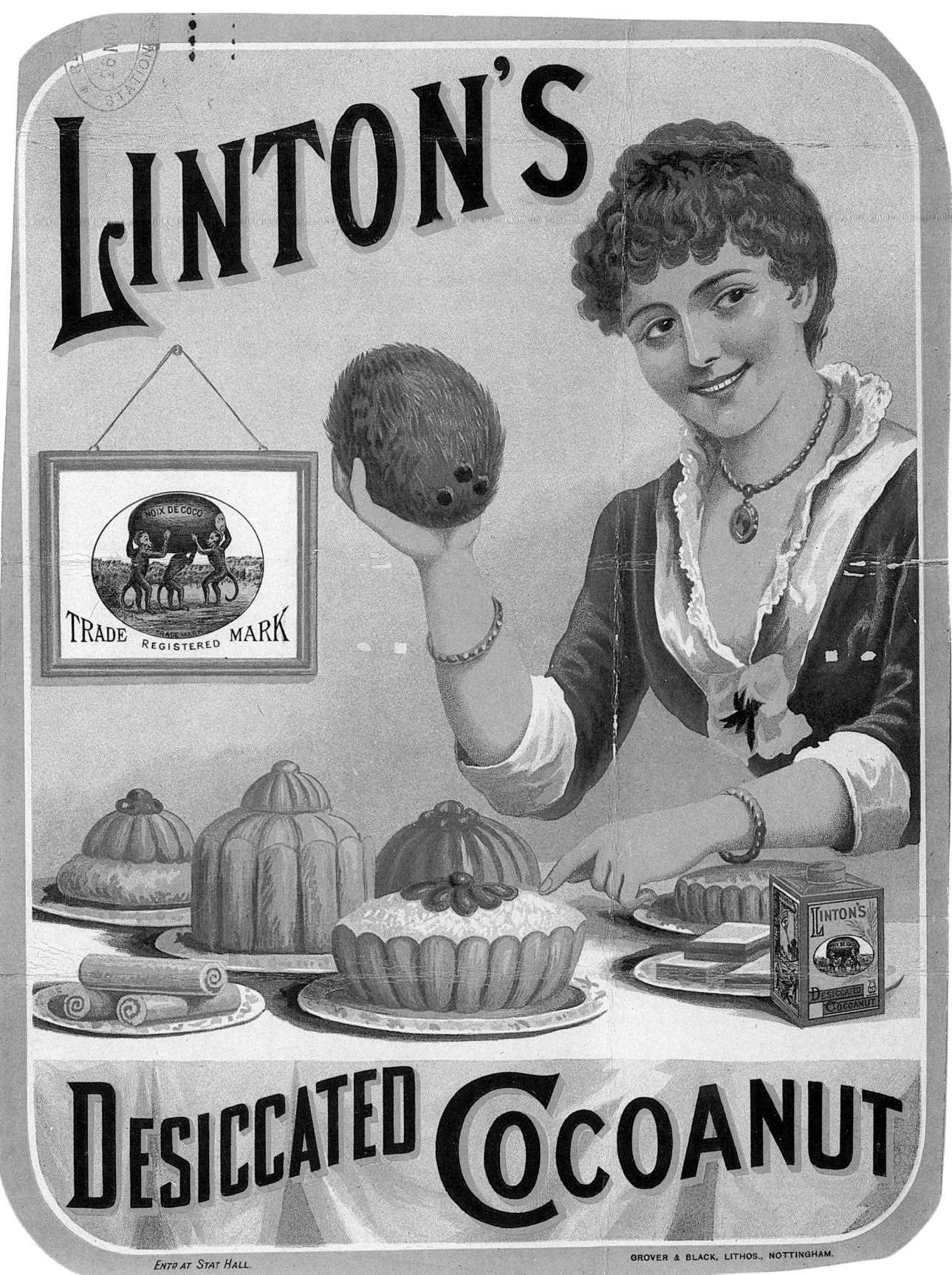

9 Linton's Desiccated Cocoanut
Date registered: 26 November 1885
Size: 24cm x 30cm

10 Lyle's Golden Syrup
Date registered: 9 September 1898
Size: 51cm x 39cm

11 Lyle's Pure Confectionery
Date registered: 9 September 1898
Size: 38cm x 51cm

388

KOHLER'S CHOCOLATES

"Worth Struggling for"

12 Kohler's Chocolates
Date registered: 4 September 1900
Size: 51cm x 38cm

13 Rowntree's Chocolates and Cocoa
Date registered: 9 August 1900
Size: 59cm x 79cm

14 Rothwell's Milk Chocolate
Date registered: 17 August 1900
Size: 35cm x 47cm

15 Danish Dairy Butter
Date registered: 31 January 1908
Size: 61cm x 91cm

16 Pleasure Brand Tea
Date registered: 27 July 1888
Size: 48cm x 35cm

17 Bellman Tea
Date registered: 16 June 1898
Size: 51cm x 76cm

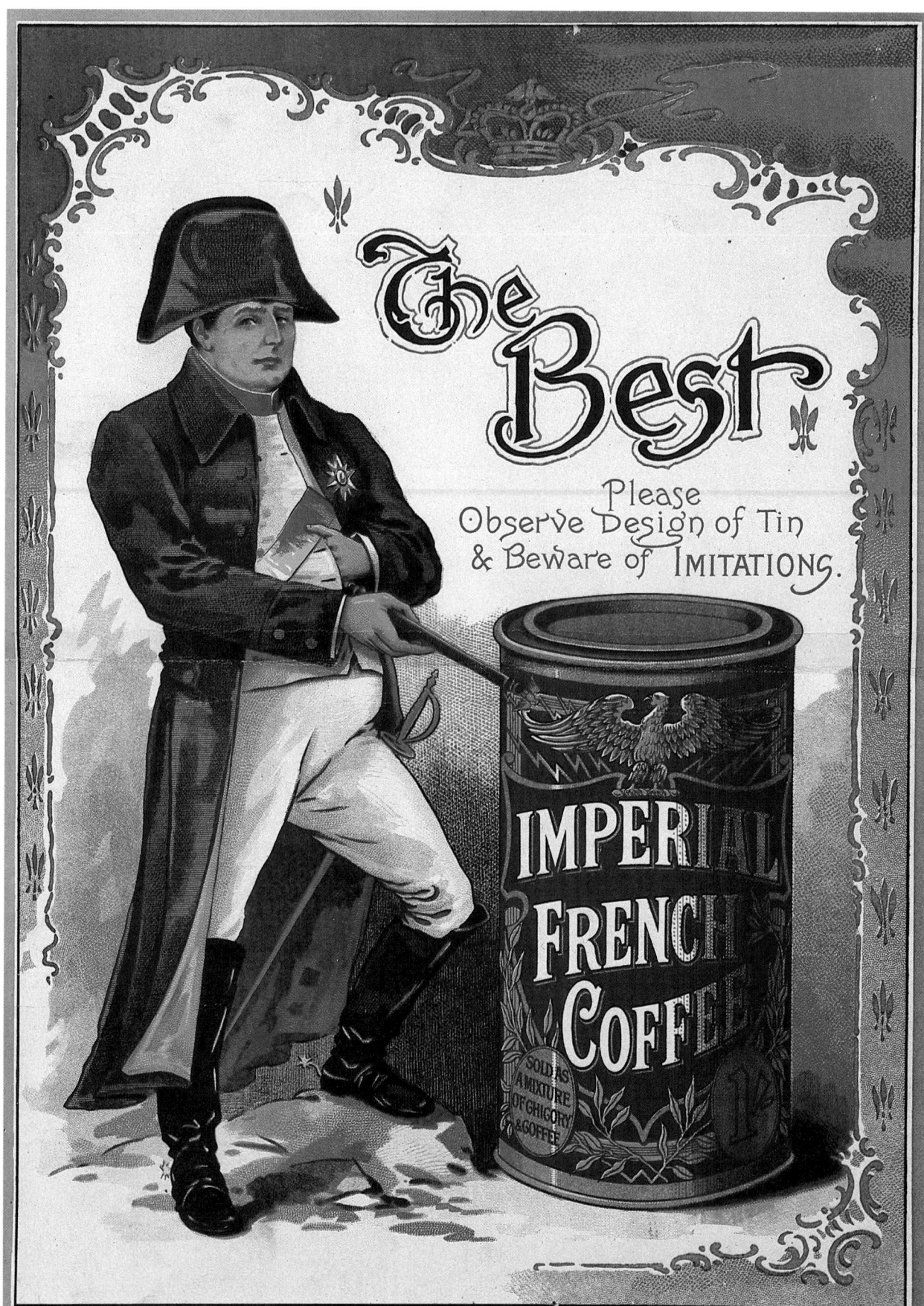

18 Imperial French Coffee
Date registered: 27 September 1898
Size: 28cm x 38cm

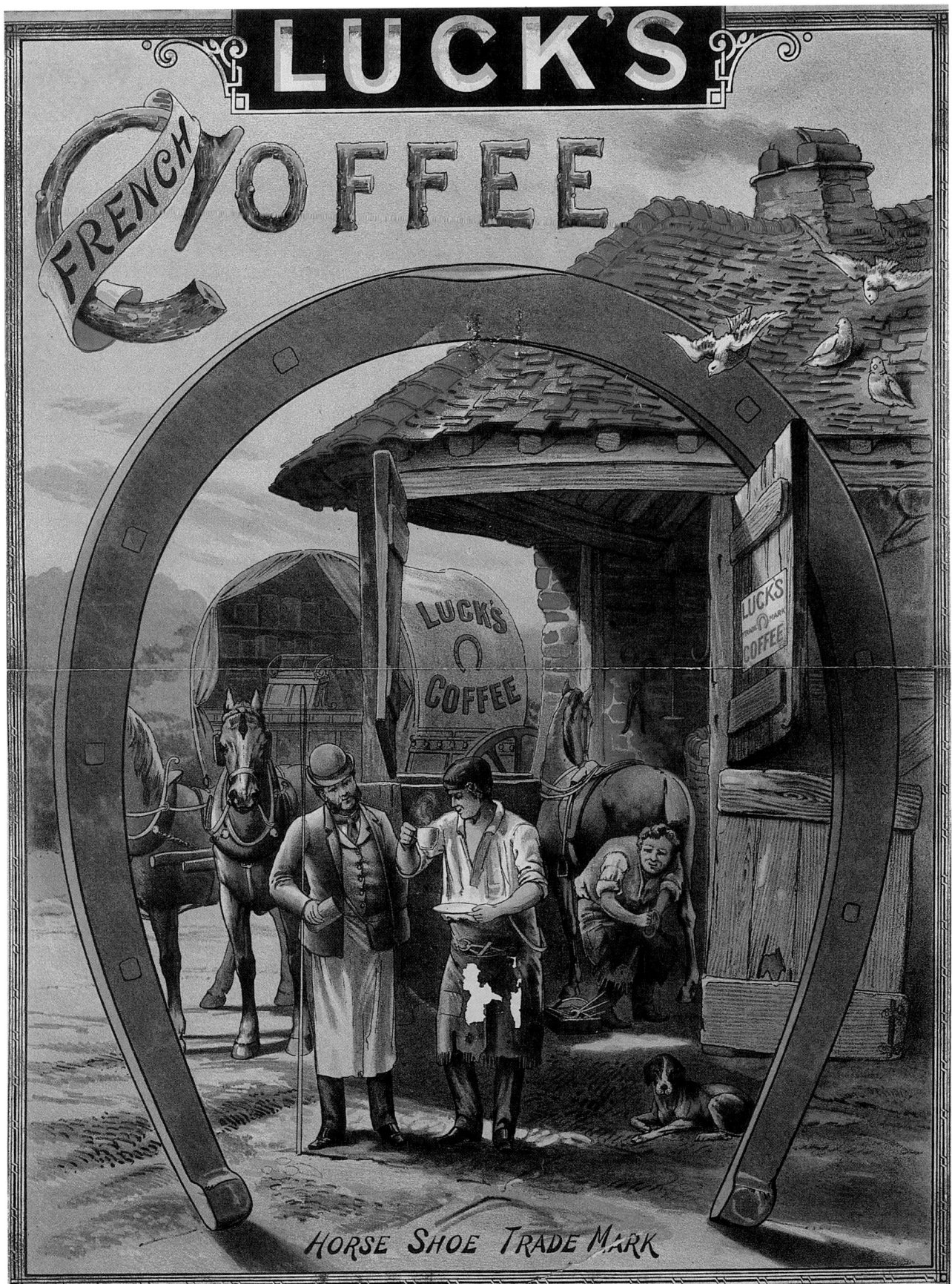

19 Luck's French Coffee
Date registered: 15 October 1885
Size: 30cm x 39cm

20 Zip Tonic Table Water
Date registered: 8 October 1907
Size: 48cm x 73cm

21 Truman's Ales and Stouts
Date registered: 28 January 1908
Size: 32cm x 47cm

22 Jacob's Pilsener Lager Beer
Date registered: 7 May 1898
Size: 55cm x 41cm

23 The Laird's Scotch Whiskey
Date registered: 2 February 1888
Size: 32cm x 49cm

24 Roderick Dhu Whisky
Date registered: 21 June 1898
Size: 37cm x 49cm

"TO THE RESCUE."

25 Martell's Brandy
Date registered: 20 December 1910
Size: 51cm x 75cm

26 Schweppes Green Ginger Wine
Date registered: 12 December 1910
Size: 51cm x 63cm

27 Ogden's Midnight Flake
Date registered: 22 November 1900
Size: 45cm x 59cm

28 Weinberg's Mahalla Cigarettes
Date registered: 21 October 1907
Size: 44cm x 57cm

29 Hadjetian Cigarettes
Date registered: 17 January 1911
Size: 53cm x 39cm

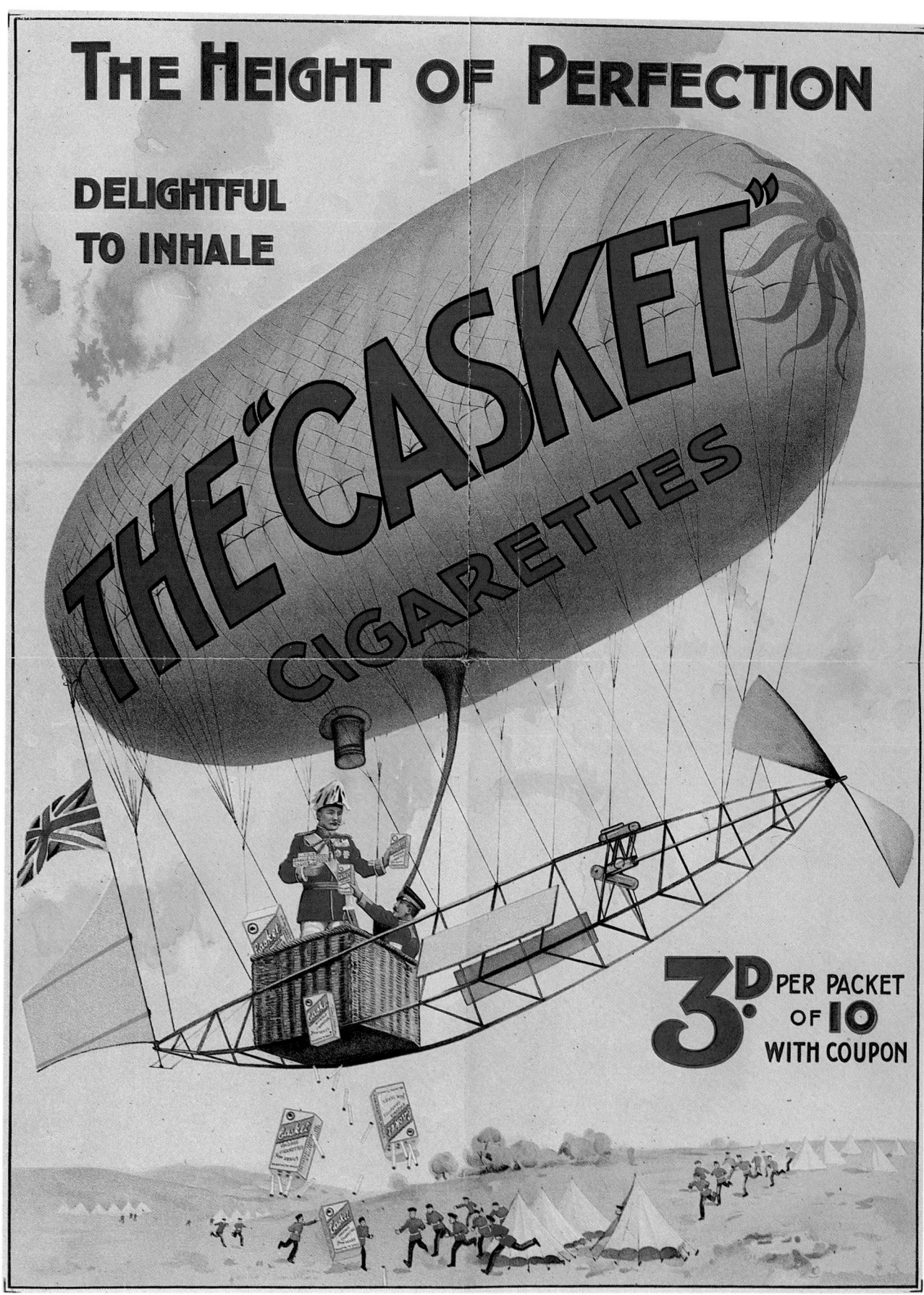

30 The 'Casket' Cigarettes
Date registered: 16 November 1907
Size: 38cm x 51cm

31 Cope's Tobaccos
Date registered: 11 May 1888
Size: 51cm x 37cm

32 Irish Pig Tail Tobacco
Date registered: 17 December 1885
Size: 29cm x 15cm

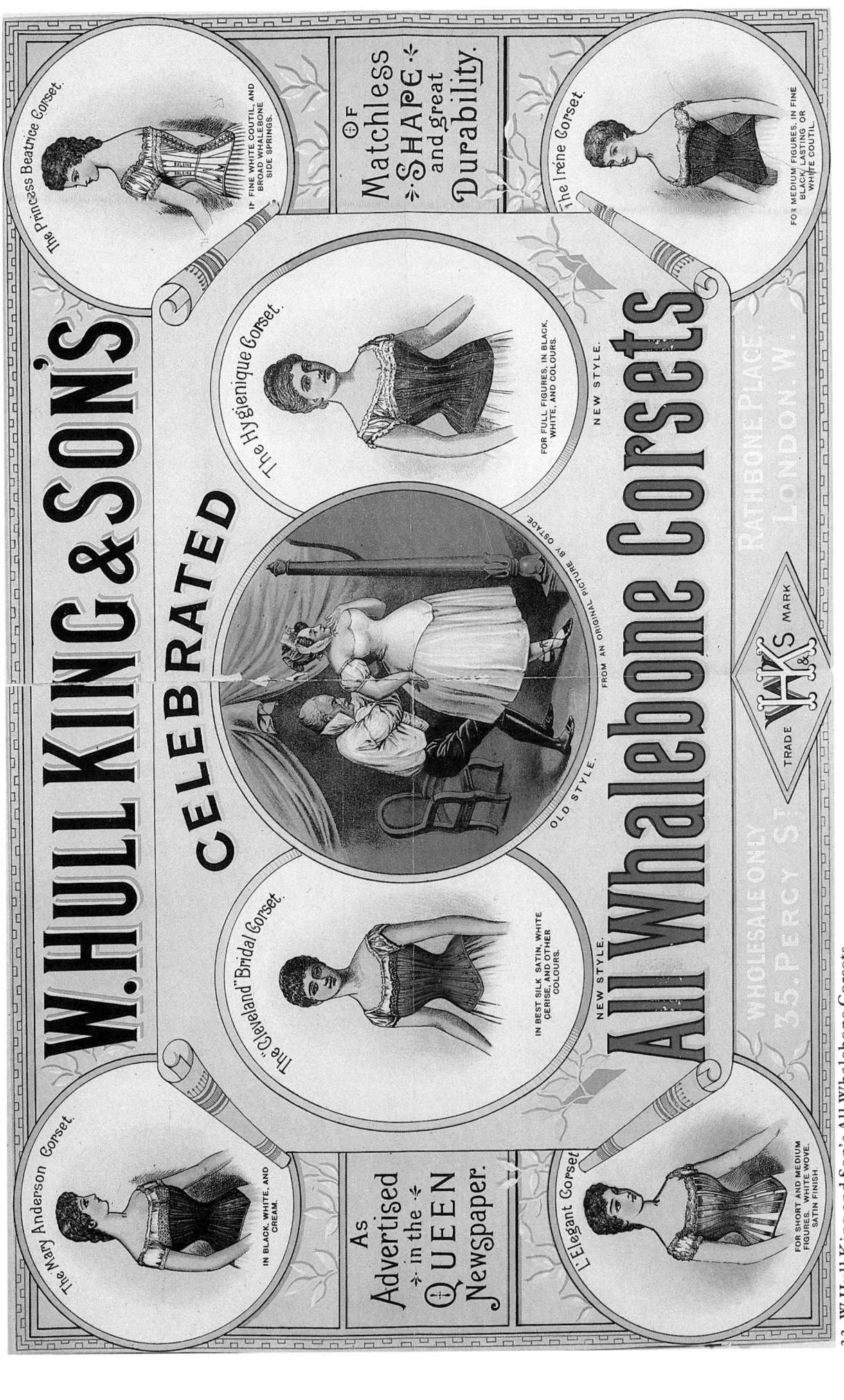

33 W Hull King and Son's All Whalebone Corsets
Date registered: 17 January 1888
Size: 47cm x 30cm

34 W F Corsets and Underclothing
Date registered: 1 October 1898
Size: 29cm x 46cm

35 The Oktis Corset Shields
Date registered: 19 August 1900
Size: 11cm x 23cm

36 The High Class Washing Flannel
Date registered: 13 October 1898
Size: 54cm x 67cm

37 The Boltonian Under-Vest
Date registered: 3 February 1888
Size: 36cm x 48cm

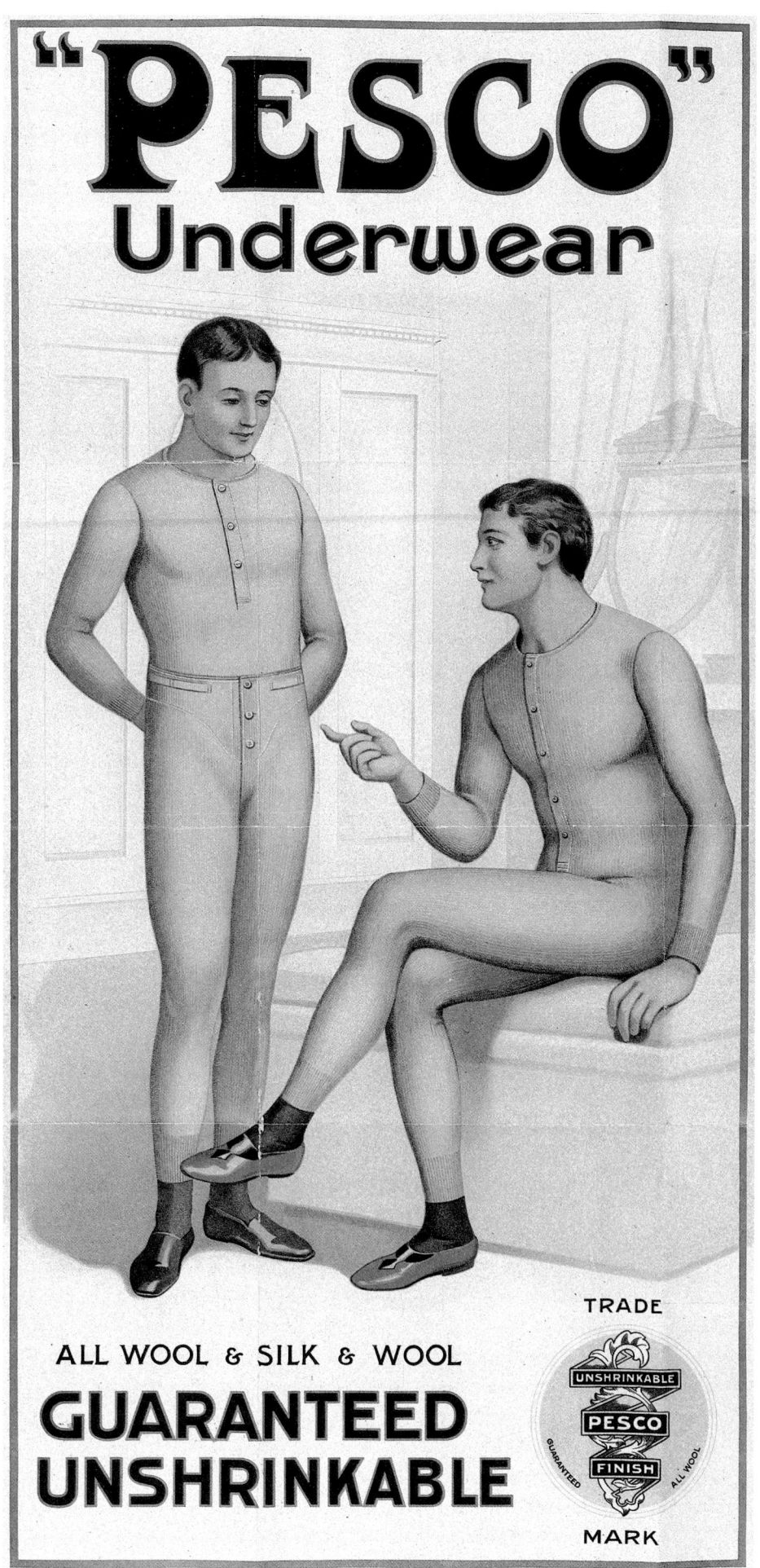

38 'Pesco' Underwear
Date registered: 7 March 1911
Size: 37cm x 62cm

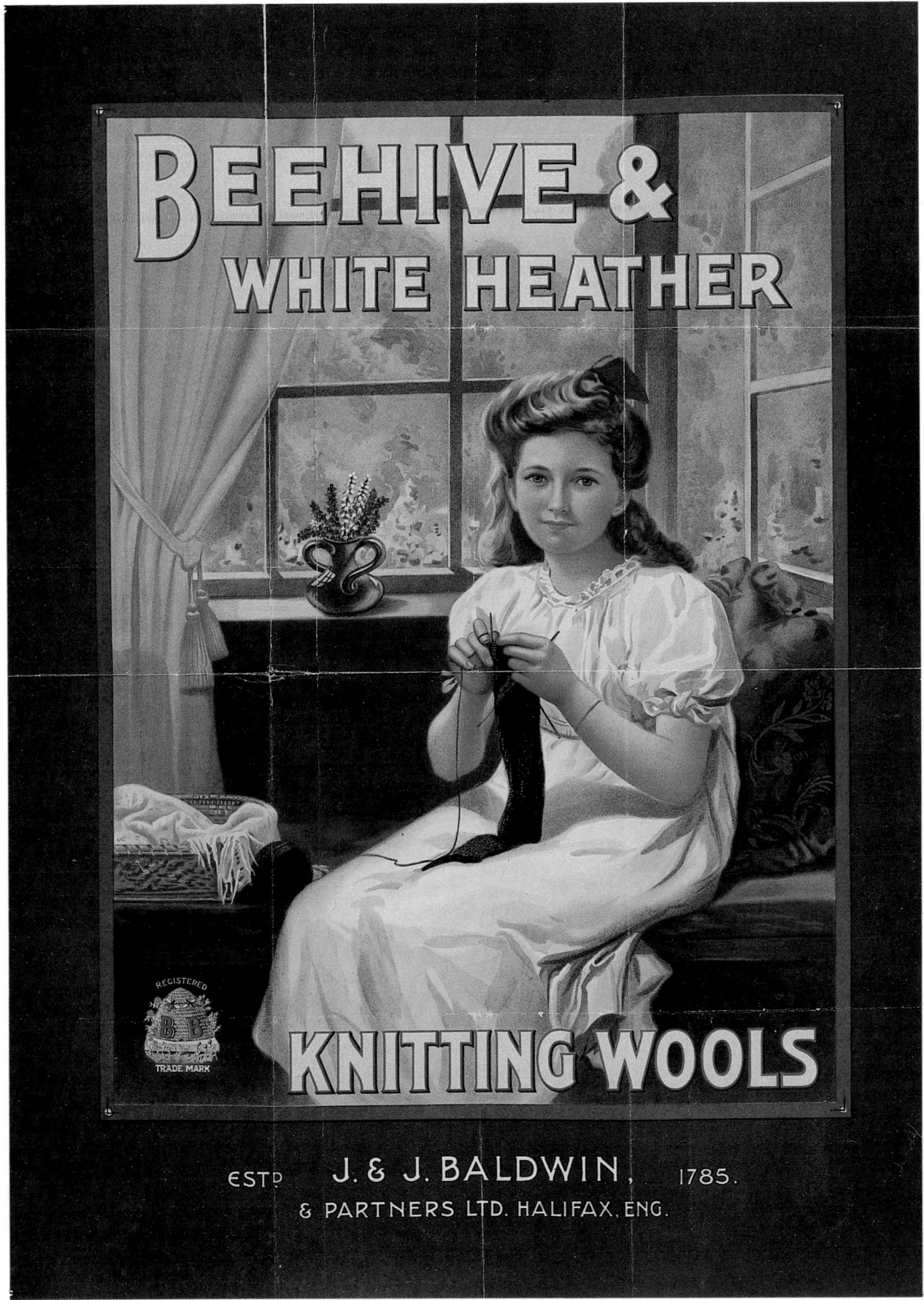

39 'Beehive' and 'White Heather' Knitting Wools
Date registered: 28 December 1910
Size: 40cm x 53cm

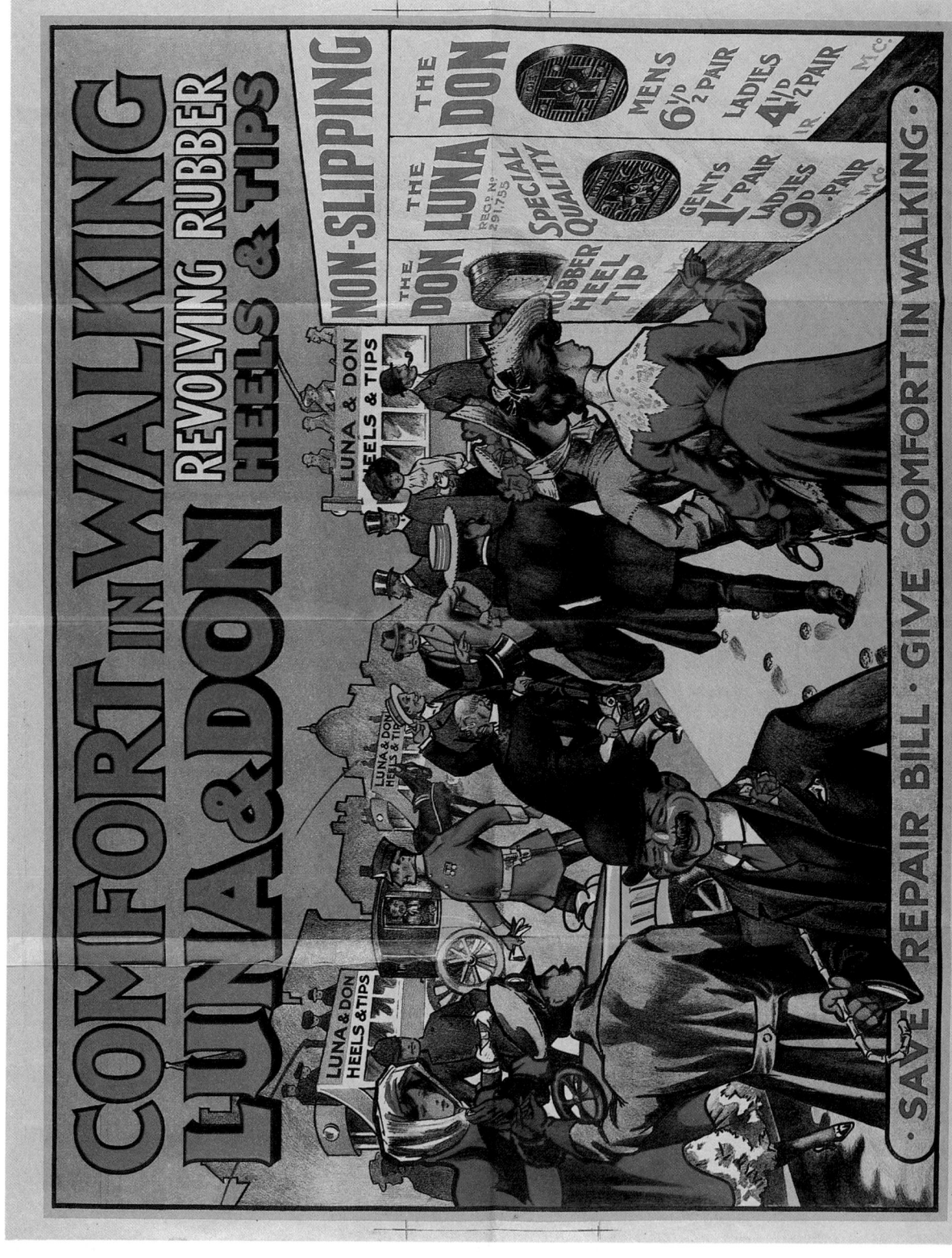

40 'The Luna' and 'The Don' Revolving Rubber Heels and Tips
Date registered: 7 September 1907
Size: 63cm x 51cm

41 'The Lady' Boots and Shoes
Date registered: 12 December 1910
Size: 37cm x 24cm

"A PROTECTED CRUISER"

BOSTON RUBBER SHOE CO.
RUBBERS.

42 Boston Rubber Shoe Company
Date registered: 16 June 1898
Size: 30cm x 65cm

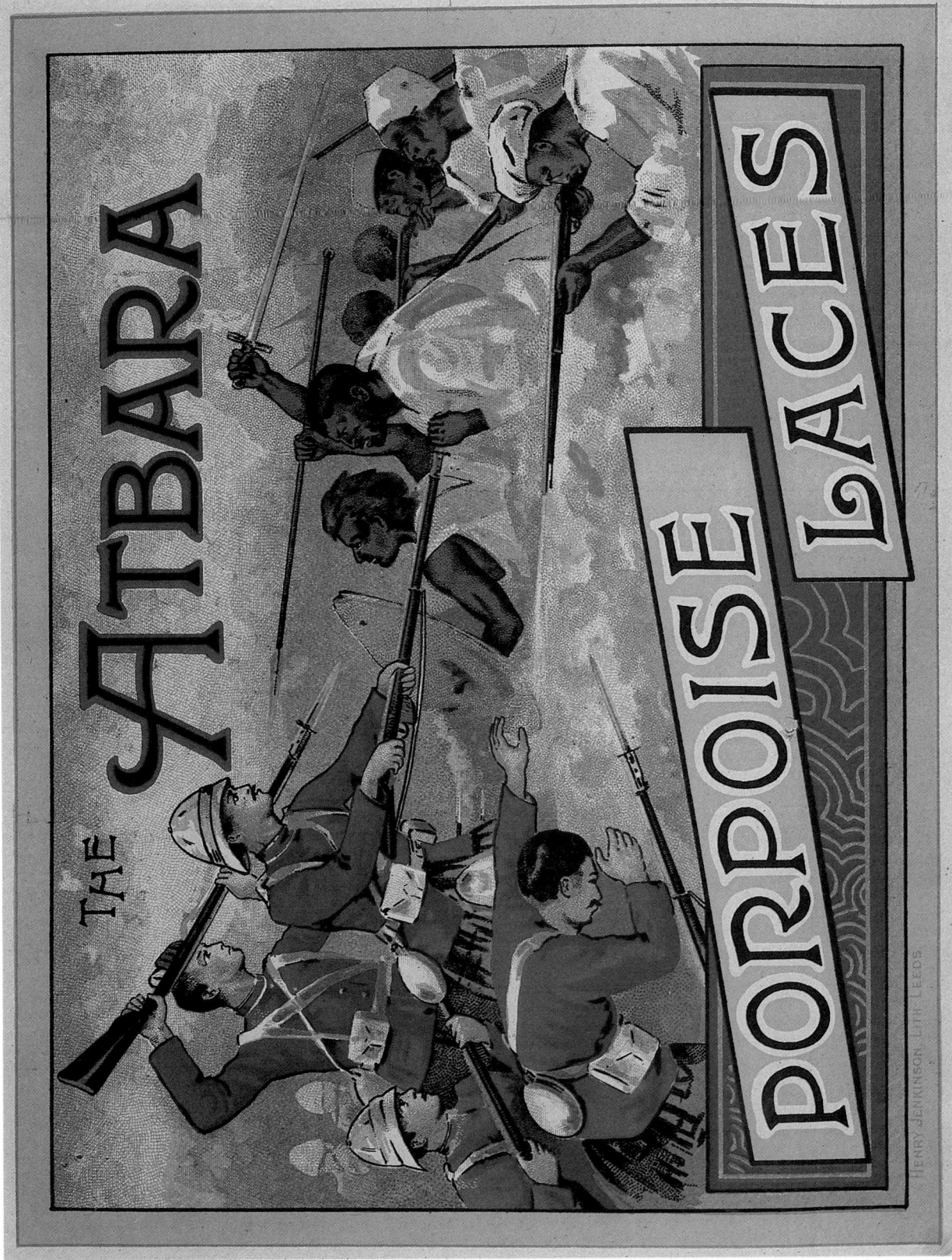

43 'Atbara' Porpoise Laces
Date registered: 15 September 1898
Size: 24cm x 18cm

44 'Concrete' Football Boots
Date registered: 2 March 1911
Size: 18cm x 26cm

45 Robert Brown's White Windsor Soap
Date registered: 13 October 1885
Size: 37cm x 48cm

46 Hudson's Extract of Soap
Date registered: 20 June 1888
Size: 36cm x 47cm

47 Watson's Matchless Cleaner
Date registered: 22 November 1898
Size: 33cm x 40cm

48 'Royd' Chauffeur Soap
Date registered: 28 October 1907
Size: 25cm x 38cm

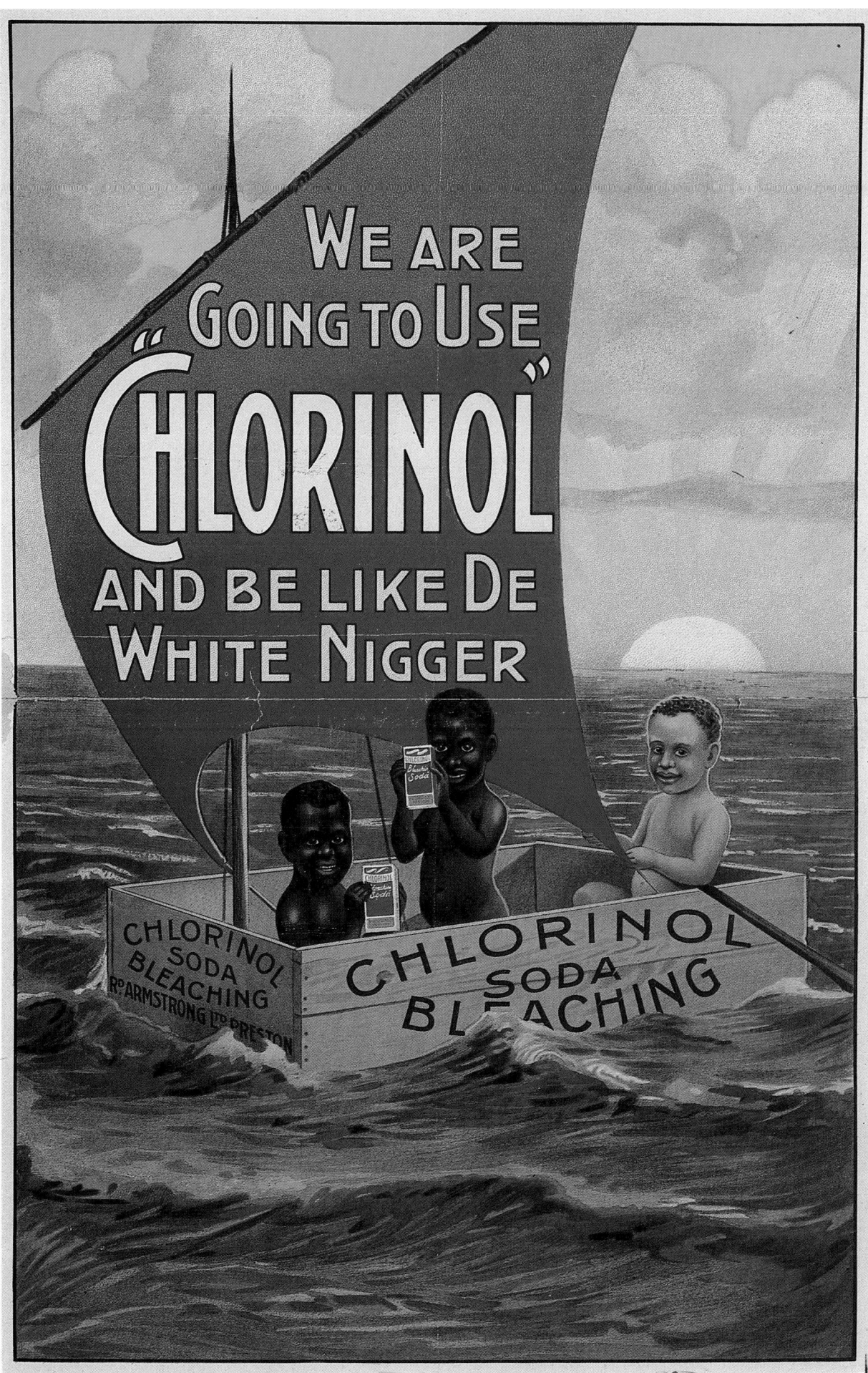

49 'Chlorinol' Soda Bleaching
Date registered: 9 December 1907
Size: 25cm x 38cm

50 'I Shine' Boot Polish
Date registered: 28 December 1910
Size: 23cm x 30cm

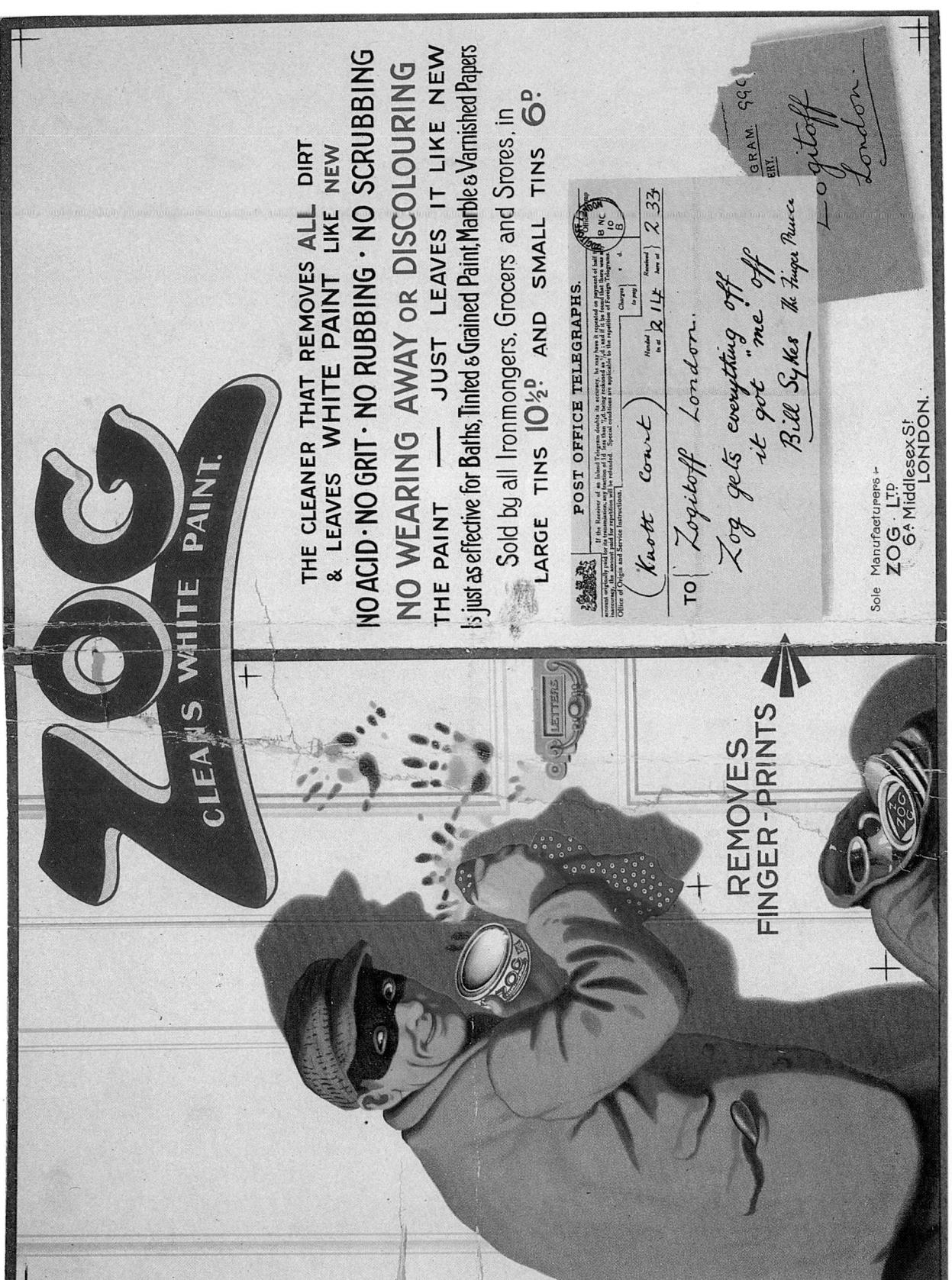

51 'Zog' Cleaner
Date registered: 11 January 1911
Size: 30cm x 23cm

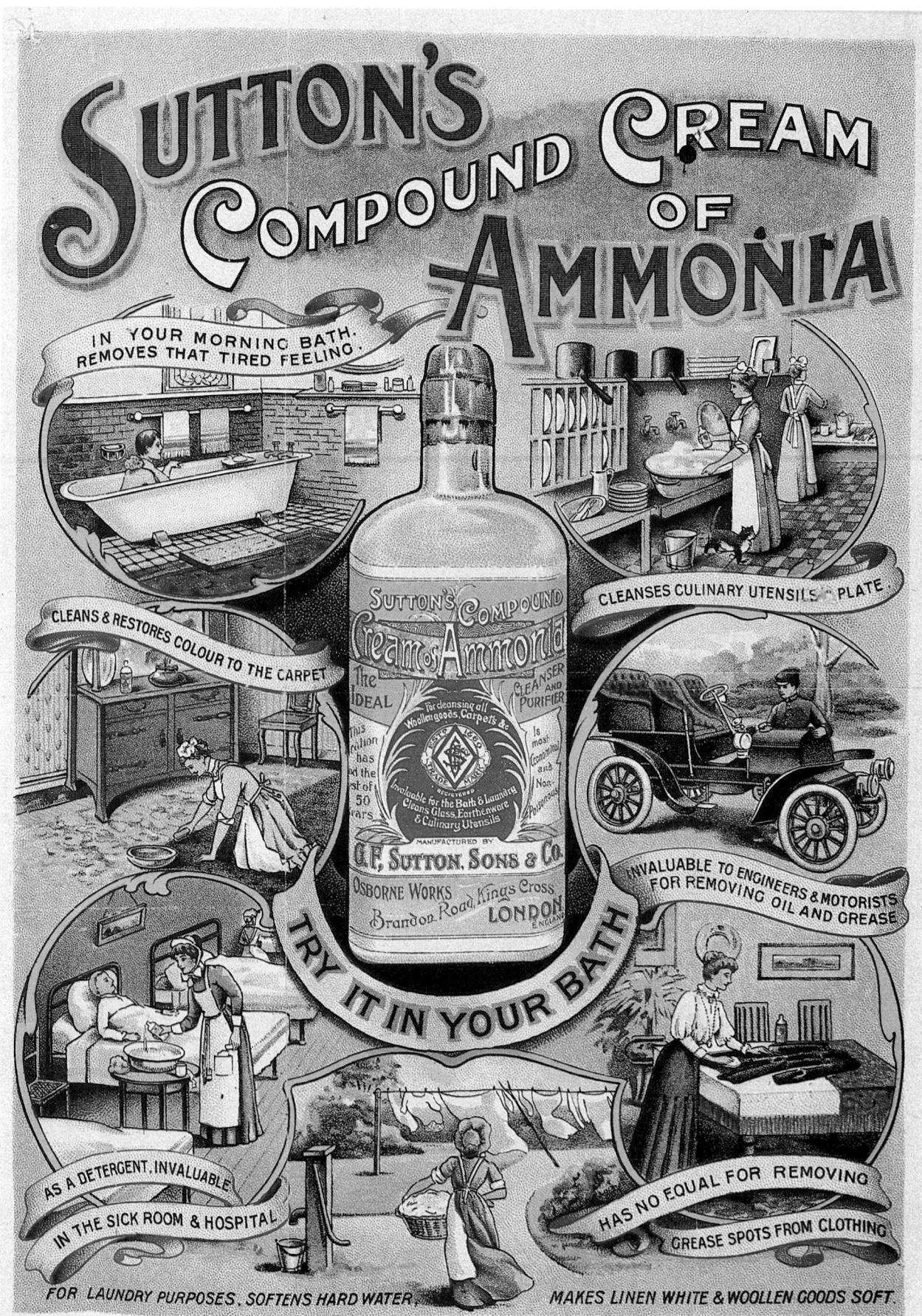

52 Sutton's Compound Cream of Ammonia
Date registered: 17 October 1907
Size: 18cm x 25cm

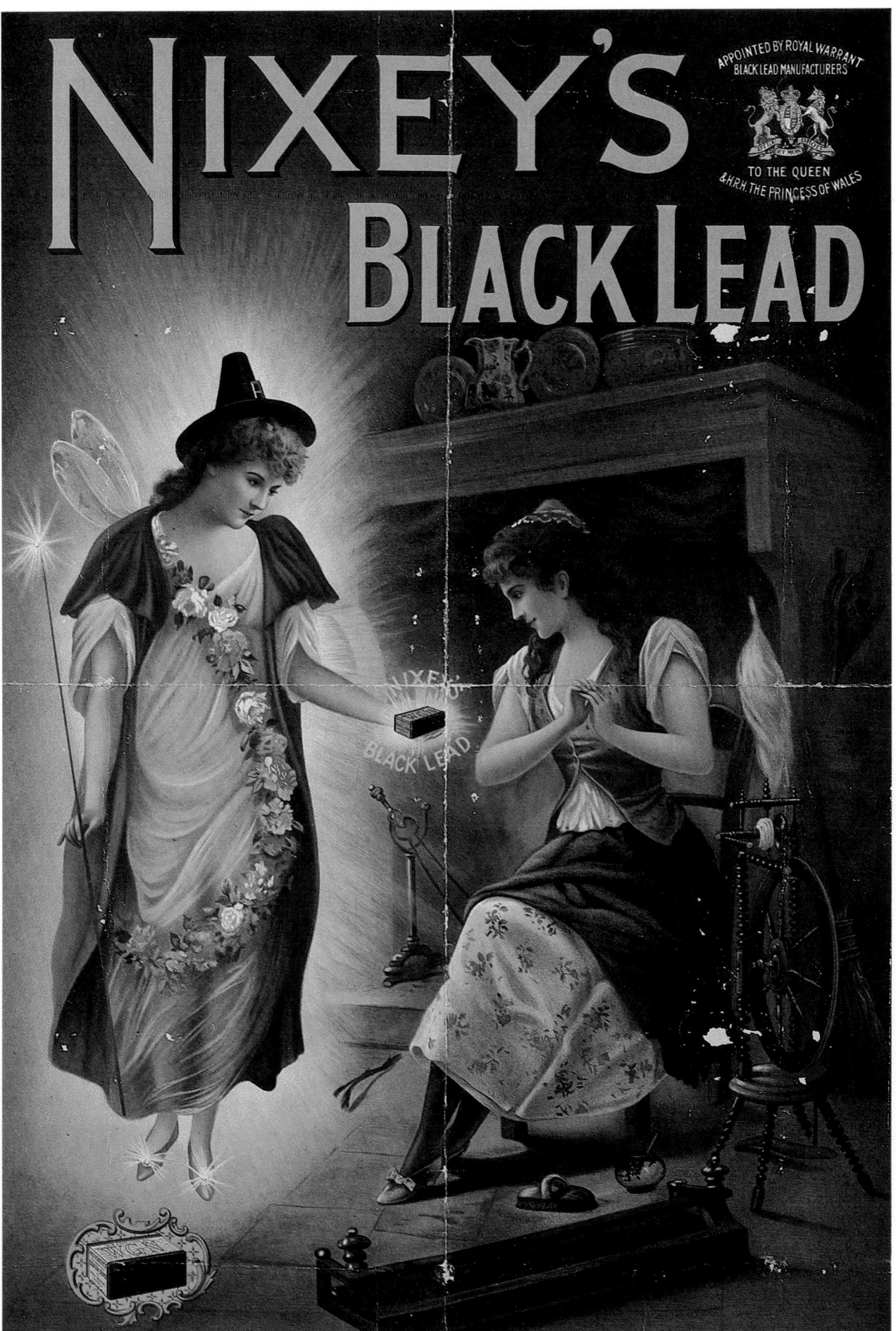

53 Nixey's Black Lead
Date registered: 20 October 1898
Size: 33cm x 47cm

54 'Komo' Furniture Cream and Black Enamel
Date registered: 27 January 1911
Size: 27cm x 40cm

55 'Esse' Anthracite Stoves
Date registered: 12 December 1910
Size: 36cm x 48cm

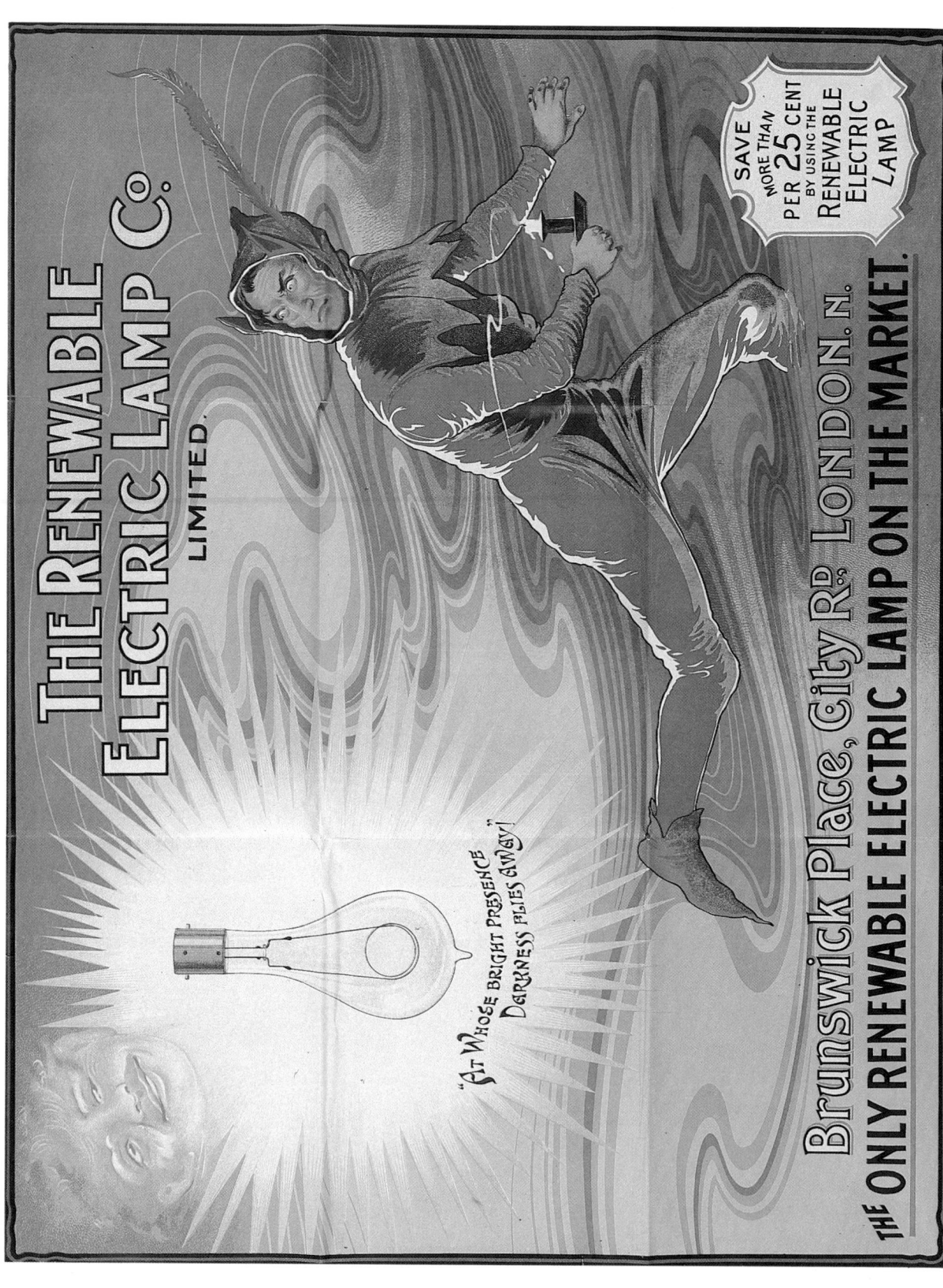

56 The Renewable Electric Lamp Company Ltd
Date registered: 12 November 1900
Size: 55cm x 44cm

57 Beecham's Pills
Date registered: 24 September 1888
Size: 22cm x 28cm

58 Buffalo's Pills
Date registered: 21 February 1888
Size: 25cm x 15cm

59 Salvo Petrolia
Date registered: 22 November 1888
Size: 17cm x 24cm

60 Kuro Company Assorted Pills
Date registered: 24 September 1907
Size: 26cm x 16cm

61 Willson's Sparkling Stomach Tonic
Date registered: 4 August 1900
Size: 65cm x 51cm

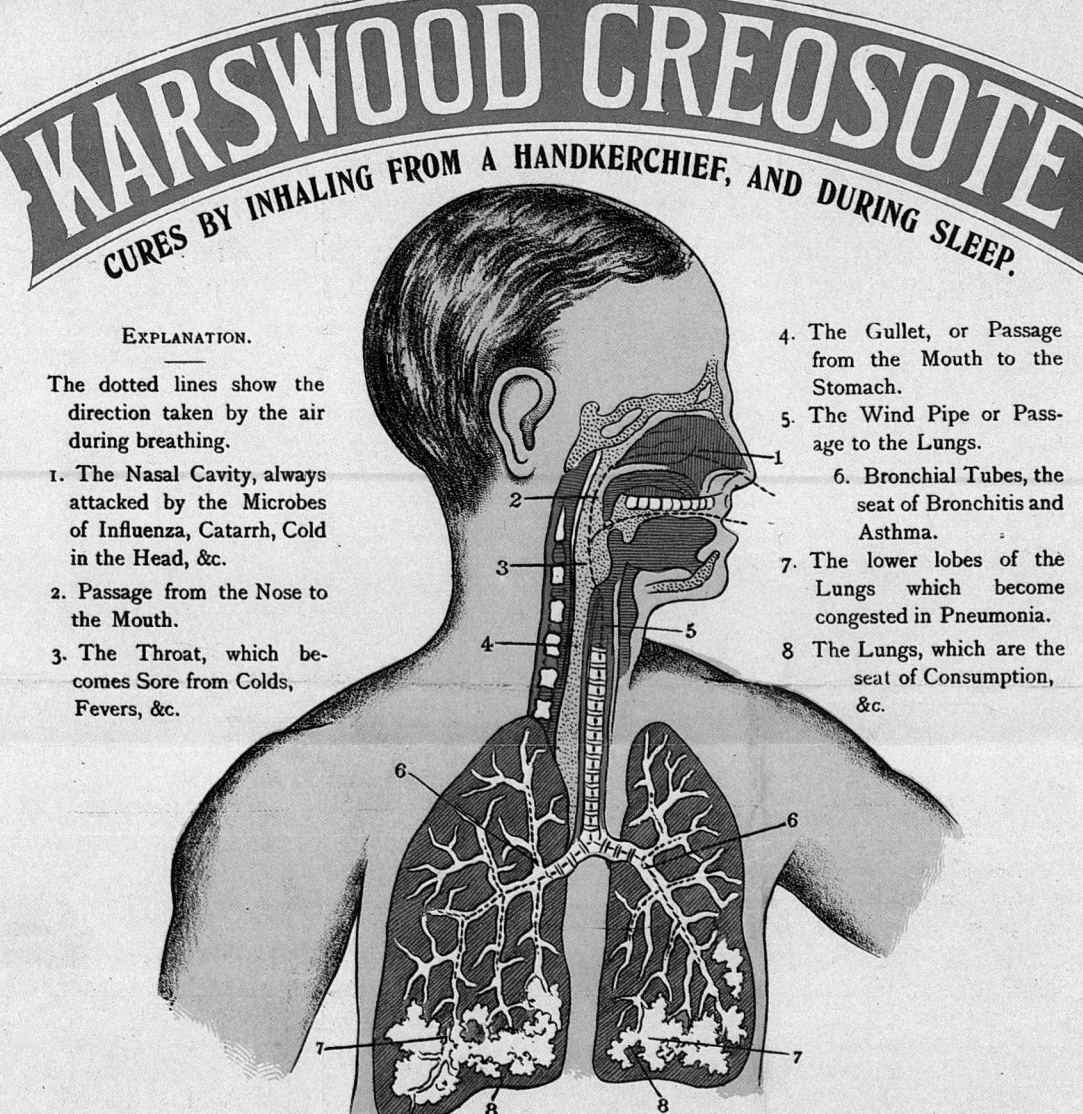

The Greatest Cure on Earth.

KARSWOOD CREOSOTE

CURES BY INHALING FROM A HANDKERCHIEF, AND DURING SLEEP.

EXPLANATION.

The dotted lines show the direction taken by the air during breathing.

1. The Nasal Cavity, always attacked by the Microbes of Influenza, Catarrh, Cold in the Head, &c.
2. Passage from the Nose to the Mouth.
3. The Throat, which becomes Sore from Colds, Fevers, &c.

4. The Gullet, or Passage from the Mouth to the Stomach.
5. The Wind Pipe or Passage to the Lungs.
6. Bronchial Tubes, the seat of Bronchitis and Asthma.
7. The lower lobes of the Lungs which become congested in Pneumonia.
8 The Lungs, which are the seat of Consumption, &c.

IT is a perfect, quick, and certain Cure for Cold in the Head, Catarrh, Influenza, Sore Throat, Bronchitis, Asthma, Whooping Cough, Croup, Incipient Consumption, Hay Fever, &c., and all Diseases affecting the Breathing Organs.

IT CURES TOOTHACHE LIKE MAGIC.

Bottles 1/1½, 2/9, 4/6 each, from all Chemists, &c.

Manufacturer :—E. GRIFFITHS HUGHES, Chemist, VICTORIA STREET, MANCHESTER.

62 Karswood Creosote
Date registered: 12 October 1898
Size: 25cm x 31cm

63 Stothert's Headache Powders
Date registered: 11 November 1900
Size: 51cm x 76cm

64 Glendenning's Beef and Malt Wine
Date registered: 24 August 1898
Size: 30cm x 40cm

Little girl — Do you use
CALVERT'S
CARBOLIC TOOTH POWDER?

65 Calvert's Carbolic Tooth Powder
Date registered: 29 August 1888
Size: 24cm x 41cm

66 Robin Starch
Date registered: 27 January 1911
Size: 28cm x 41cm

TOM MERRY, DEL ET LITH. 102 & 104 NEWINGTON BUTTS, LONDON. S.E

67 **Menotti, the Stockholm Wonder High Telephone Wire Cyclist**
Date registered: 25 February 1889
Size: 71cm x 49cm

68 Dan Leno at the London Pavilion
Date registered: 30 October 1900
Size: 47cm x 71cm

69 The Biograph
Date registered: 30 October 1900
Size: 43cm x 70cm

70 Sheffield Dog Show
Date registered: 5 October 1885
Size: 57cm x 44cm

71 Pain's Electric Fireworks
Date registered: 20 August 1900
Size: 19cm x 27cm

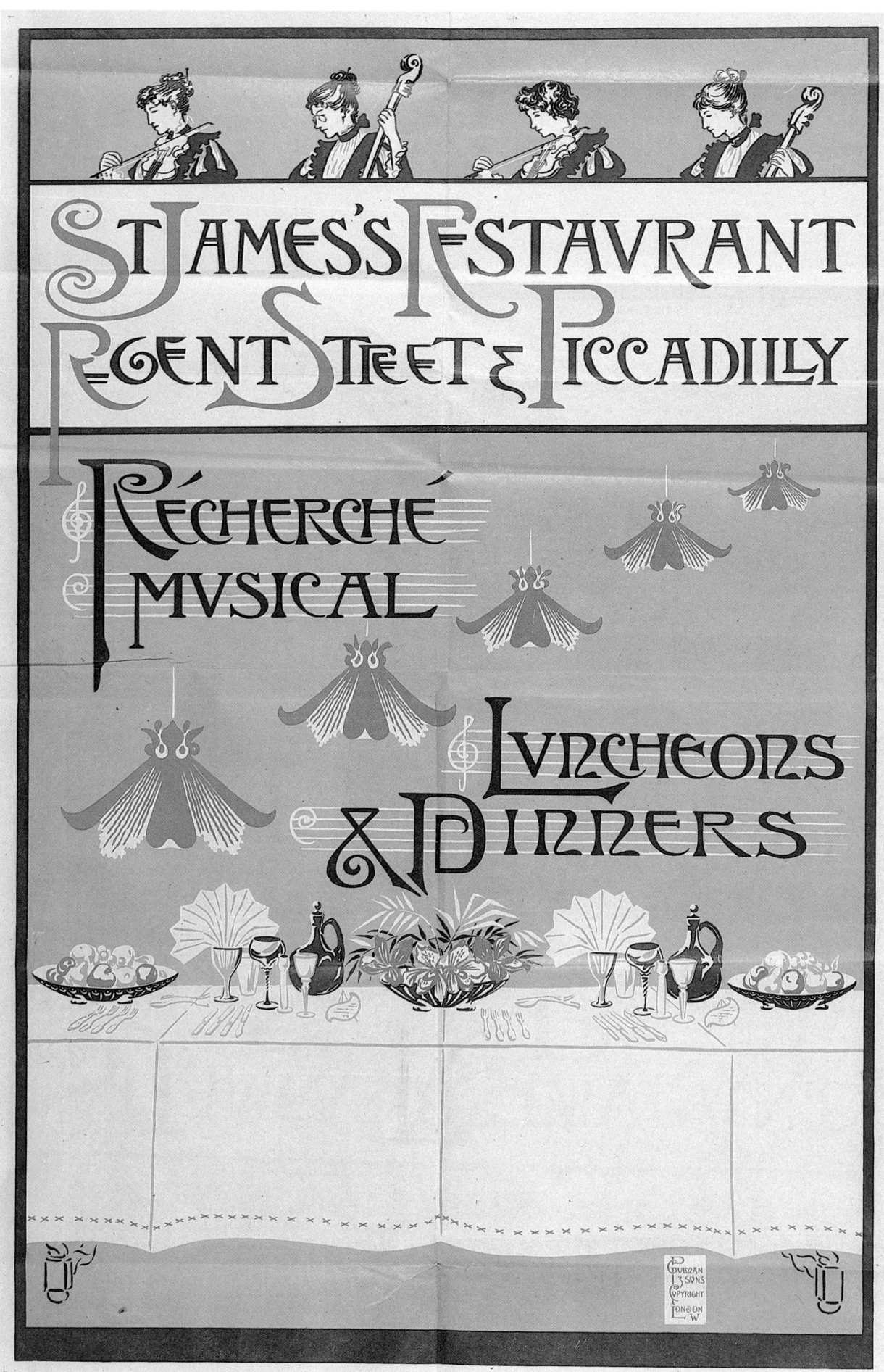

72 St James's Restaurant, Regent Street and Piccadilly
Date registered: 15 December 1898
Size: 57cm x 88cm

73 Atlas Puncture Proof Inner Case
Date registered: 9 March 1911
Size: 38cm x 51cm

74 Palmer Tyres
Date registered: 19 December 1898

75 The Safety Skirt Holder
Date registered: 27 May 1898
Size: 33cm x 22cm

76 Spinner Linton and Company
Date registered: 15 October 1907
Size: 22cm x 28cm

77 All One
Date registered: 24 September 1900
Size: 56cm x 61cm

78 In Memoriam
Date registered: 26 September 1900
Size: 51cm x 76cm

79 Using the National Army
Date registered: 21 September 1900
Size: 51cm x 76cm

80 East London Water Consumers' Defence Association
Date registered: 19 September 1898
Size: 44cm x 57cm

Food and Drink

1 Edwards' Desiccated Soup
Registered by: Samuel Herbert Benson, 1 Tudor Street, London EC
Copyright assigned to: Stewart and Woolf
Author: Julius Aberle, 410 Birkbeck Bank Chambers, Chancery Lane, London WC
Date registered: 19 September 1900
PRO reference: COPY 1/170 folio 146
Size: 26cm x 33cm

2 Holbrook's Sauce
Registered by: Howard and Jones, 15 and 16 Cullum Street, London EC
Author: Joseph Widgery, 25 Bury Street, London EC
Date registered: 4 November 1898
PRO reference: COPY 1/144 folio 338
Size: 20cm x 29cm

3 Royal Wilts Bacon
Registered by: Bennett Brothers Ltd, Counterslip, Bristol
Author: Samuel Ernest Cox, 63 Kennington Avenue, Bishopston, Bristol
Date registered: 8 January 1908
PRO reference: COPY 1/265 folio 336
Size: 53cm x 38cm

4 Liebig's Extract of Meat
The picture depicts Queen Victoria, attended by (from right to left) the Marquis of Salisbury, Mr Gladstone, the Duke of Cambridge, Lord Charles Beresford and the Archbishop of Canterbury.
Registered by: Liebig's Extract of Meat Company Ltd, 9 Fenchurch Avenue, London EC
Author: Robert Dudley, 31 Lansdowne Road, Notting Hill, London W
Date registered: 30 August 1888
PRO reference: COPY 1/83 folio 136
Size: 58cm x 30cm

5 Cerebos Salt
Registered by: Tom Browne and Company, Boulevard Printing Works, Lenton, Nottingham
Author: Tom Browne, 'Woolaton', Hardy Road, Westcombe Park, London SE
Date registered: 19 December 1898
PRO reference: COPY 1/145 folio 161
Size: 26cm x 39cm

6 Coomb's Eureka Aerated Pastry Flour
Registered by: William Augustus Coomb, St Ann's Well Road, Nottingham
Copyright assigned to: Grover and Black, Davis Street, Nottingham
Author: Charles Frederick Thompson, 70 Blue Bell Hill, Nottingham
Date registered: 11 May 1888
PRO reference: COPY 1/82 folio 232
Size: 37cm x 24cm

7 Borwick's Baking Powder
Registered by: Nathaniel Lloyd and Company, 81 Queen Victoria Street, London EC
Author: Alfred Howell Moore, c/o Nathaniel Lloyd and Company
Date registered: 25 July 1898
PRO reference: COPY 1/142 folio 65
Size: 39cm x 52cm

8 Brown and Polson's Corn Flour
Registered by: Nathaniel Lloyd and Company, 81 Queen Victoria Street, London EC
Author: Richard Oswald Allen, c/o Nathaniel Lloyd and Company
Date registered: 9 August 1900
PRO reference: COPY 1/169 folio 241
Size: 51cm x 39cm

9 Linton's Desiccated Cocoanut
Registered by: Linton Hubbard and Company, 18 and 19 Red Lion Square, London WC
Copyright assigned to: Grover and Black, Davis Street, Carlton Road, Nottingham
Author: Charles Frederick Thompson, Blue Bell Hill, Nottingham
Date registered: 26 November 1885
PRO reference: COPY 1/71 folio 11 Size: 24cm x 30cm

10 Lyle's Golden Syrup
Registered by: Abram Lyle and Sons Ltd, 21 Mincing Lane, London EC
Author: Miss Emma Heatley, 21 Norland Square, London W and Edwin James Clemitson, 20 Bury Street, London EC
Date registered: 9 September 1898
PRO reference: COPY 1/143 folio 269
Size: 51cm x 39cm

11 Lyle's Pure Confectionery
Registered by: Abram Lyle and Sons Ltd, 21 Mincing Lane, London EC
Author: Miss Emma Heatley, 21 Norland Square, London W
Date registered: 9 September 1898
PRO reference: COPY 1/143 folio 270
Size: 38cm x 51cm

12 Kohler's Chocolates
Registered by: Nathaniel Lloyd and Company, 81 Queen Victoria Street, London EC
Author: Alfred Howell Moore, c/o Nathaniel Lloyd and Company
Date registered: 4 September 1900
PRO reference: COPY 1/170 folio 387
Size: 51cm x 38cm

13 Rowntree's Chocolates and Cocoa
Registered by: Samuel Herbert Benson, 1 Tudor Street, London EC
Copyright assigned to: McCorquodale and Company Ltd
Author: Joseph Littler, 31 Penn Road Villas, Holloway, London N
Date registered: 9 August 1900
PRO reference: COPY 1/169 folio 253
Size: 59cm x 79cm

14 Rothwell's Milk Chocolate
Registered by: Albert Hildesheimer, 2 New Zealand Avenue, Barbican, London EC
Author: Howard Davie, Romany Rest, Gipsy Lane, Barnes Common, London SW
Date registered: 17 August 1900
PRO reference: COPY 1/169 folio 179
Size: 35cm x 47cm

15 Danish Dairy Butter
Registered by: George Jamieson, 132 Constitution Street, Leith, Scotland
Author: Christopher George Oseman, 312 Abbeydale Road, Sheffield (of Woollen and Company, Sheffield)
Date registered: 31 January 1908
PRO reference: COPY 1/265 folio 38
Size: 61cm x 91cm

16 Pleasure Brand Tea
Registered by: W Turner and Company, 12 Fenchurch Street, London EC
Author: John Thomas Greenslade, employed by Harmer and Harley, 220 Upper Thames Street, London EC
Date registered: 27 July 1888
PRO reference: COPY 1/87 folio 384
Size: 48cm x 35cm

17 Bellman Tea
Registered by: The Liverpool Printing and Stationery Company Ltd, 42 Castle Street, Liverpool
Author: Charles Douglas Mackenzie, 28 Falkner Street, Liverpool
Date registered: 16 June 1898
PRO reference: COPY 1/142 folio 211
Size: 51cm x 76cm

18 Imperial French Coffee
Registered by: Brodie, Williams and Boyes Ltd, 6 and 7 Cross Lane, Eastcheap, London EC
Author: Fisher Edkins, 64 Holte Road, Aston, Birmingham
Date registered: 27 September 1898
Size: 28cm x 38cm

19 Luck's French Coffee
Registered by: Samuel Hanson, Son and Barter, 47 Botolph Lane, London EC
Author: James Horner, 49 Calthorpe Street, Gray's Inn Road, London WC
Date registered: 15 October 1885
PRO reference: COPY 1/70 folio 54
Size: 30cm x 39cm

20 Zip Tonic Table Water
Registered by: Nathaniel Lloyd and Company, Burrell Street Works, Blackfriars, London SE
Author: Alfred Nicholls, c/o Nathaniel Lloyd and Company
Date registered: 8 October 1907
PRO reference: COPY 1/262 folio 15
Size: 48cm x 73cm

Alcohol and Tobacco

21 Truman's Ales and Stouts
Registered by: Nathaniel Lloyd and Company, Burrell Street Works, London SE
Author: Francis Smith, c/o Nathaniel Lloyd and Company
Date registered: 28 January 1908
PRO reference: COPY 1/265 folio 33
Size: 32cm x 47cm

22 Jacob's Pilsener Lager Beer
Registered by: Frederick Jacob and Company, 77 Theobald's Road, London
Copyright assigned to: Raphael Tuck and Sons Ltd
Author: Edwin Hughes, 13 Hebron Road, The Grove, Hammersmith, London W
Date registered: 7 May 1898
PRO reference: COPY 1/84 folio 283
Size: 55cm x 41cm

23 The Laird's Scotch Whiskey
Registered by: E Lindsey Pembroke, 20 Jewry Street, Aldgate, London EC
Author: Chadwick Rymer, 2 Warton Street, King's Cross Road, London WC
Date registered: 2 February 1888
PRO reference: COPY 1/81 folio 367
Size: 32cm x 49cm

24 Roderick Dhu Whisky
Registered by: Tom Browne and Company, Boulevard Printing Works, Lenton, Nottingham
Author: Tom Browne, 'Woolaton', Hardy Road, Westcombe Park, London SE
Date registered: 21 June 1898
PRO reference: COPY 1/142 folio 139
Size: 37cm x 49cm

25 Martell's Brandy
Registered by: David Allen and Sons Ltd, 17 Leicester Street, London
Author: Ernest Anson Dyer, 105 Kingsley Avenue, West Ealing
Date registered: 20 December 1910
PRO reference: COPY 1/301 folio 123
Size: 51cm x 75cm

26 Schweppes Green Ginger Wine
Registered by: Nathaniel Lloyd and Company Ltd., Burrell Street Works, Blackfriars, London SE
Author: Alfred William Pearce, c/o Nathaniel Lloyd and Company
Date registered: 12 December 1910
PRO reference: COPY 1/301 folio 332
Size: 51cm x 63cm

27 Ogden's Midnight Flake
Registered by: Thomas Forman and Sons, Sherwood Street, Nottingham
Copyright assigned to: Henry Moran, 29 Burchington Road, Kilburn, London NW
Author: Henry Moran
Date registered: 22 November 1900
PRO reference: COPY 1/172 folio 372
Size: 45cm x 59cm

28 Weinberg's Mahalla Cigarettes
Registered by: The London Printing Alliance Ltd, Grafton Works, North Road, Holloway, London N
Author: Frederick Taylor, employed by The London Printing Alliance Ltd
Date registered: 21 October 1907
PRO reference: COPY 1/262 folio 202
Size: 44cm x 57cm

29 Hadjetian Cigarettes
Registered by: Apet Hadjetian, Esbekieh, Cairo, Egypt
Author: William Ernest Bradbury, 91 Fernlea Road, Balham, London SW
Date registered: 17 January 1911
PRO reference: COPY 1/302 folio 237
Size: 53cm x 39cm

30 The 'Casket' Cigarettes
Registered by: P A Baumann and Company Ltd, 33–34 Shoe Lane, London EC
Author: Howard David Ebberleigh, Lingfield Avenue, Kingston-upon-Thames
Date registered: 16 November 1907
PRO reference: COPY 1/263 folio 254
Size: 38cm x 51cm

31 Cope's Tobaccos
Registered by: Cope Brothers and Company Ltd, 10 Lord Nelson Street, Liverpool
Assigned to: John Wallace, 11 Melbourne Place, Edinburgh
Author: John Wallace
Date registered: 11 May 1888
PRO reference: COPY 1/82 folio 230
Size: 51cm x 37cm

32 Irish Pig Tail Tobacco
Registered by: Frederick Allen and Sons, Canal Road,
Mile End, London
Author: Henry Johnson, Arkwright Street, Nottingham
Date registered: 17 December 1885
PRO reference: COPY 1/72 folio 30
Size: 29cm x 15cm

Clothing and Shoes

33 W Hull King and Son's All Whalebone Corsets
Registered by: W Hull King and Son, 35 Percy Street,
Rathbone Place, London W
Author: W Hull King, Elleray, 40 Newstead Road,
Lee, Kent
Date registered: 17 January 1888
PRO reference: COPY 1/81 folio 446
Size: 47cm x 30cm

34 W F Corsets and Underclothing
Registered by: William Fletcher Ltd, Landport Street,
Landport, Portsmouth
Author: George Haigh, 10 Southfield Square, Bradford
Date registered: 1 October 1898
PRO reference: COPY 1/144 folio 413
Size: 29cm x 46cm

35 The Oktis Corset Shields
Registered by: Albert Hildesheimer, 2 New Zealand
Avenue, Barbican, London EC
Author: Victor Venner, 13 Elm Grove, Cricklewood,
London NW
Date registered: 19 August 1900
PRO reference: COPY 1/169 folio 192
Size: 11cm x 23cm

36 The High Class Washing Flannel
Registered by: George Adolphus Woodward and John
Charles Edwards, trading as Leopold
Schwarbacker, 4a Bread Street,
London EC
Author: George Henry Taylor, 63 Wiltshire Road,
Brixton, London SW
Date registered: 13 October 1898
PRO reference: COPY 1/144 folio 273
Size: 54cm x 67cm

37 The Boltonian Under-Vest
Registered by: William Rothwell, 1 Market Street,
Bolton
Author: William Rothwell
Date registered: 3 February 1888
PRO reference: COPY 1/81 folio 343
Size: 36cm x 48cm

38 'Pesco' Underwear
Registered by: P A Baumann and Company Ltd,
33–34 Shoe Lane, London EC
Author: Thomas Kinsella, 26 Farrah Street,
Vassall Road, Brixton, London SW
Date registered: 7 March 1911
PRO reference: COPY 1/304 folio 219
Size: 37cm x 62cm

39 'Beehive' and 'White Heather' Knitting Wools
Registered by: P A Baumann and Company Ltd.,
33–34 Shoe Lane, London EC
Author: Robert Hunter, 50 Wolseley Avenue,
Wimbledon Park, London SW
Date registered: 28 December 1910
PRO reference: COPY 1/301 folio 51
Size: 40cm x 53cm

40 'The Luna' and 'The Don' Revolving Rubber Heels and Tips
Registered by: Sam Clarke, 41 Granby Row, Manchester
Author: Edward Bryan, 56 Rigby Street, Higher
Broughton, Manchester
Date registered: 7 September 1907
PRO reference: COPY 1/261 folio 317
Size: 63cm x 51cm

41 'The Lady' Boots and Shoes
Registered by: Nathaniel Lloyd and Company Ltd.,
Burrell Street Works, Blackfriars,
London SE
Author: Alfred William Pearce, c/o Nathaniel Lloyd
and Company
Date registered: 12 December 1910
PRO reference: COPY 1/301 folio 334
Size: 37cm x 24cm

42 Boston Rubber Shoe Company
Registered by: John Wood Knott, trading as Boston
Rubber Shoe Company, 47 Farringdon
Street, London EC and Boston USA
Author: John Wood Knott
Date registered: 16 June 1898
PRO reference: COPY 1/142 folio 199
Size: 30cm x 65cm

43 'Atbara' Porpoise Laces
The poster depicts the Battle of Atbara, on 8 April
1898, at which Kitchener defeated an army of 18,000
Sudanese dervishes.
Registered by: Henry Jenkinson, Chestnut Avenue,
Victoria Road, Leeds
Author: Henry Jenkinson
Date registered: 15 September 1898
PRO reference: COPY 1/143 folio 197
Size: 24cm x 18cm

44 'Concrete' Football Boots
Registered by: Thomas Henry Crumbie, Halford Street,
Leicester
Author: Harold Whittaker, 161 Harrow Road, Leicester
Date registered: 2 March 1911
PRO reference: COPY 1/304 folio 296 Size: 18cm x 26cm

Cleaning, Blacking, Heat and Light

45 Robert Brown's White Windsor Soap
The poster depicts Queen Victoria, Mr Gladstone and the
Marquis of Salisbury
Registered by: Robert Brown and Company, 29 Back
Piccadilly, Manchester
Author: Edward Palmer, Talton Street,
Ashton under Lyme
Date registered: 13 October 1885
PRO reference: COPY 1/71 folio 110 Size: 37cm x 48cm

46 Hudson's Extract of Soap
Registered by: Arnold Thomas and Edward Caddick,
trading as R S Hudson, Bank Hall,
Liverpool
Author: William Jones, the W J Factory, Off Golden
Lane, London EC
Date registered: 20 June 1888
PRO reference: COPY 1/82 folio 22 Size: 36cm x 47cm

47 Watson's Matchless Cleaner
Registered by: Joseph Watson and Sons Ltd, Whitehall
Soap Works, Leeds
Author: Howard Davie, Romany Rest, Gipsy Lane,
Putney, London SW
Date registered: 22 November 1898
PRO reference: COPY 1/144 folio 130 Size: 33cm x 40cm

48 'Royd' Chauffeur Soap
Registered by: Albert Hildesheimer and Son, Coventry House, South Place, London EC
Author: Vernon Barrett, 50 Stavordale Road, Highbury, London N
Date registered: 28 October 1907
PRO reference: COPY 1/262 folio 89 Size: 25cm x 38cm

49 'Chlorinol' Soda Bleaching
Registered by: P A Baumann and Company Ltd, 33–34 Shoe Lane, London EC
Author: Howard Davie, Ebberleigh, Lingfield Avenue, Kingston-upon-Thames
Date registered: 9 December 1907
PRO reference: COPY 1/264 folio 294
Size: 25cm x 38cm

50 'I Shine' Boot Polish
Registered by: P A Baumann and Company Ltd, 33–34 Shoe Lane, London EC
Author: Thomas Kinsella, 26 Farrah Street, Vassall Road, Brixton, London SW
Date registered: 28 December 1910
PRO reference: COPY 1/301 folio 53
Size: 23cm x 30cm

51 'Zog' Cleaner
Registered by: P A Baumann and Company Ltd, 33–34 Shoe Lane, London EC
Author: Thomas Kinsella, 26 Farrah Street, Vassall Road, Brixton, London SW
Date registered: 11 January 1911
PRO reference: COPY 1/302 folio 326
Size: 30cm x 23cm

52 Sutton's Compound Cream of Ammonia
Registered by: G F Sutton, Sons and Company, Osborne Works, Brandon Road, Kings Cross, London N
Author: William John Wilkins, Norwich Road, Ipswich
Date registered: 17 October 1907
PRO reference: COPY 1/262 folio 253
Size: 18cm x 25cm

53 Nixey's Black Lead
Registered by: Thomas Forman and Sons, Sherwood Street, Nottingham
Author: Faustin Betbeder, Foxley Road, North Brixton, London
Date registered: 20 October 1898
PRO reference: COPY 1/144 folio 153
Size: 33cm x 47cm

54 'Komo' Furniture Cream and Black Enamel
Registered by: Nathaniel Lloyd and Company Ltd, Burrell Street Works, Blackfriars, London SE
Author: Alexander Strahan Buchanan, c/o Nathaniel Lloyd and Company
Date registered: 27 January 1911
PRO reference: COPY 1/302 folio 65
Size: 27cm x 40cm

55 'Esse' Anthracite Stoves
Registered by: Nathaniel Lloyd and Company Ltd, Burrell Street Works, Blackfriars, London SE
Author: Alfred William Pearce, c/o Nathaniel Lloyd and Company
Date registered: 12 December 1910
PRO reference: COPY 1/301 folio 333
Size: 36cm x 48cm

56 The Renewable Electric Lamp Company Ltd
Registered by: Howard Jones, 16 Cullum Street, London EC
Author: Wilson Smith, Lawrence Pountney Lane, London EC
Date registered: 12 November 1900
PRO reference: COPY 1/172 folio 161
Size: 55cm x 44cm

Pills and Potions

57 Beecham's Pills
Registered by: Thomas Beecham, St Helens, Lancashire
Author: Edmund George Turnbull, 5 South Hill Park Gardens, Hampstead
Date registered: 24 September 1888
PRO reference: COPY 1/83 folio 29
Size: 22cm x 28cm

58 Buffalo's Pills
Registered by: Jackson and Hoyle, Bacup, Lancashire
Author: John Bailey, 28 Gloster Street, Bolton
Date registered: 21 February 1888
PRO reference: COPY 1/81 folio 197
Size: 25cm x 15cm

59 Salvo Petrolia
Registered by: The Dee Oil Company Ltd, Saltney, Chester
Author: Henry Moran, 7 Eaton Terrace, St John's Wood, London NW
Date registered: 22 November 1888
PRO reference: COPY 1/84 folio 379
Size: 17cm x 24cm

60 Kuro Company Assorted Pills
Registered by: Ann Cowood, trading as Kuro Company, Grey Walk Passage, Hunslet, Leeds
Author: Benson Baxter, 27 Park Cross Street, Leeds
Date registered: 24 September 1907
PRO reference: COPY 1/126 folio 63
Size: 26cm x 16cm

61 Willson's Sparkling Stomach Tonic
Lord Roberts became a national hero after his victories at Bloemfontein, Mafeking, and Pretoria in early 1900
Registered by: William Anthony Willson, Canal Street, Nottingham
Author: Arthur Smith, 15 Kinglake Street, Nottingham
Date registered: 4 August 1900
PRO reference: COPY 1/169 folio 309
Size: 65cm x 51cm

62 Karswood Creosote
Registered by: Evan Griffiths Hughes, Victoria Street, Manchester
Author: Lily Grundy Hughes, 6 John Dalton Street, Manchester
Date registered: 12 October 1898
PRO reference: COPY 1/144 folio 298
Size: 25cm x 31cm

63 Stothert's Headache Powders
Registered by: Hind, Hoyle and Light Ltd, Britannia Works, East Street, Lr Mosley Street, Manchester
Author: Henry Hammond Light, 7 Northern Grove, West Didsbury, Manchester
Date registered: 11 November 1900
PRO reference: COPY 1/172 folio 236
Size: 51cm x 76cm

64 Glendenning's Beef and Malt Wine
Registered by: Albert Hildesheimer, 2 New Zealand
Avenue, London EC
Author: Howard Davie, Romany Rest, Gipsy Lane,
Putney, London SW
Date registered: 24 August 1898
PRO reference: COPY 1/143 folio 86
Size: 30cm x 40cm

65 Calvert's Carbolic Tooth Powder
Registered by: F C Calvert and Company, Bradford
Author: William Lynch, 15 Distillery Street, Belfast
Date registered: 29 August 1888
PRO reference: COPY 1/83 folio 187
Size: 24cm x 41cm

66 Robin Starch
Registered by: Nathaniel Lloyd and Company Ltd,
Burrell Street Works, Blackfriars,
London SE
Author: John Dumayne, Alexander Strahan Buchanan
and Leopold John Wells, c/o Nathaniel Lloyd
and Company
Date registered: 27 January 1911
PRO reference: COPY 1/302 folio 57
Size: 28cm x 41cm

Leisure and Entertainment

**67 Menotti, the Stockholm Wonder High Telephone
Wire Cyclist**
Registered by: Otto Menotti, 40 Trinity Road, Bootle,
Liverpool
Author: Tom Merry, 102 Newington Butts, London SE
Date registered: 25 February 1889
PRO reference: COPY 1/85 folio 194
Size: 71cm x 49cm

68 Dan Leno at the London Pavilion
Registered by: Weiners Ltd, Wybert Street, Munster
Square, London NW
Author: Alick Penrose and Forbes Ritchie, 21 Hornton
Street, Kensington, London W
Date registered: 30 October 1900
PRO reference: COPY 1/171 folio 263
Size: 47cm x 71cm

69 The Biograph
Registered by: Weiners Ltd, Wybert Street, Munster
Square, London NW
Author: James William Elwell Page, 3 Cambridge Road,
Barnes, London SW
Date registered: 30 October 1900
PRO reference: COPY 1/171 folio 261
Size: 43cm x 70cm

70 Sheffield Dog Show
Registered by: Walter Kelsey Taunton, 86 Hatton
Garden, London EC
Author: Walter Kelsey Taunton
Date registered: 5 October 1885
PRO reference: COPY 1/70 folio 85
Size: 57cm x 44cm

71 Pain's Electric Fireworks
Registered by: James Pain and Sons, 121 Walworth
Road, London SE
Author: Edward Henry Kirby, 12 Park Place,
New York, USA
Date registered: 20 August 1900
PRO reference: COPY 1/169 folio 148
Size: 19cm x 27cm

72 St James's Restaurant, Regent Street and Piccadilly
Registered by: George Pulman and Sons, 24–26 Thayer
Street, London W
Author: Henry Pulman, 24 Thayer Street, London W
Date registered: 15 December 1898
PRO reference: COPY 1/145 folio 213
Size: 57cm x 88cm

73 Atlas Puncture Proof Inner Case
Registered by: The London Printing Alliance, Grafton
Works, North Road, Holloway,
London N
Author: Frank Matthew Barton, employed by the
London Printing Alliance
Date registered: 9 March 1911
PRO reference: COPY 1/304 folio 195
Size: 38cm x 51cm

74 Palmer Tyres
Registered by: The Palmer Tyre Ltd, 15 Martineau
Street, Birmingham
Author: George William Harvey, 24 Underhill Road,
Lordship Lane, London SE
Date registered: 19 December 1898
PRO reference: COPY 1/145 folio 166
Size: 59cm x 44cm

75 The Safety Skirt Holder
Registered by: Charles Dawson, 23 Ilminster Gardens,
Lavender Hill, London SW
Author: Harry Parkinson, 14 Upper Street, Leeds
Date registered: 27 May 1898
PRO reference: COPY 1/142 folio 313
Size: 33cm x 22cm

76 Spinner Linton and Company
Spinner Linton were shipping agents in Manchester. For
what purpose they used this picture – described upon
registration as a 'semi-nude fairy riding a bicycle in the
clouds, dropping flowers from one hand and holding a
wand in the other hand' – is not clear.
Registered by: Spinner Linton, 11 Albert Square,
Manchester
Author: Thomas Warburton, Daisy Villa, Park Road,
Ashton on Mersey, Cheshire
Date registered: 15 October 1907
PRO reference: COPY 1/262 folio 266
Size: 22cm x 28cm

Politics

77 All One
Registered by: Edward Rice and Company, 7 St John's
Lane, Smithfield, London EC
Author: Alfred William Pearce, 38 Dalmore Road,
West Dulwich, London SE
Date registered: 24 September 1900
PRO reference: COPY 1/170 folio 90
Size: 56cm x 61cm

78 In Memoriam
The cartoon shows Sir Henry Campbell Bannerman
weeping at the grave of the Liberal Party.
Registered by: Hind, Hoyle and Light Ltd, Britannia
Works, East Street, Lower Mosley Street,
Manchester
Author: Charles Samuel Roodhouse, working for
Hind, Hoyle and Light Ltd and residing at
53 Gill Street, Blackley, Manchester
Date registered: 26 September 1900
PRO reference: COPY 1/170 folio 31
Size: 51cm x 76cm

79 Using the National Army
The poster shows Lord Salisbury supported on Lord
Roberts' shoulder distributing doles to parson and
landlord. Chamberlain declines to assist a figure
representing old age pensions. Balfour patronises
the publicans.
Registered by: John Doherty, 1 Temple Chambers,
Temple Avenue, London EC
Author: Charles Alexander Fesch, 10 Chapel Court,
Bedford Row, London WC
Date registered: 21 September 1900
PRO reference: COPY 1/170 folio 112
Size: 51cm x 76cm

80 East London Water Consumers' Defence Association
Registered by: George William Malby and Company,
Grove Crescent, Stratford, London E
Author: William Younger Calder, 12 Dangan Road,
Wanstead, Essex
Date registered: 19 September 1898
PRO reference: COPY 1/143 folio 165
Size: 44cm x 57cm

Cover
Root's Cuca Cocoa
Registered by: Adolph Henry Chamberlyn, 1 Russell
Chambers, Bloomsbury, London WC
Author: Albert Morrow, 31 Sutherland Street,
London SW
Date registered: 4 October 1888
PRO reference: COPY 1/84 folio 318
Size: 51cm x 76cm